WHAT'S NEXT?

A Perceptive Study of the "End Times" and Christ's Second Coming

FROM THE
JIMMY MORGAN EVANGELISTIC ASSOCIATION
P. O. BOX 820429
FORT WORTH, TEXAS 76182-0429

C. E. Colton

*Dedicated to the memory of Lois,
my beloved wife of 58 years,
now with the Lord in heaven*

© Copyright 1995. C. E. Colton. All rights reserved.
ISBN 0-9646448-0-0
Cover design by Jim York
Produced by JM Productions, Brentwood, Tennessee

PRINTED IN THE UNITED STATES OF AMERICA

CONTENTS

Introduction v

PART I: THE ESCHATOLOGY OF JESUS 1
Chapter 1: The End of the World 3
Chapter 2: The Great Tribulation 13
Chapter 3: The Appearance of False Christs 23
Chapter 4: The Return of Christ 31
Chapter 5: The Final Judgment 39
Chapter 6: Another Picture of the Return of Christ 49

PART II: THE ESCHATOLOGY OF PAUL 55
Chapter 7: The Christian Dead and the Second Coming . 57
Chapter 8: The Man of Sin 67
Chapter 9: The Resurrection of the Body 75

PART III: THE ESCHATOLOGY OF PETER 85
Chapter 10: The End Is at Hand 87
Chapter 11: The Delay of the Second Coming 93
Chapter 12: The Prospect of the Second Coming 99
Chapter 13: The Issues of the Second Coming 107

PART IV: THE ESCHATOLOGY OF JOHN 113
Chapter 14: The Last Hour 115
Chapter 15: Eschatology in the Apocalypse 123
Chapter 16: The Composite Picture 133

Footnotes 137

INTRODUCTION

All of us have enough sheer curiosity that we want to know all we can about the future. It is good, though, that we do not know some things about the future. On the other hand, it is expedient for us to know something of the broad outline of future events so we may be properly prepared for them.

The Bible makes it possible for us to do this. So long as we stay within the bounds of general events and principles, we are on safe and profitable ground in our interpretation of this area of biblical truth. Some, however, have allowed themselves to run wild in all sorts of fanciful interpretations far removed from the simple meanings that the biblical writers intended for them to have.

In this study we will be dealing with the primary passages of the New Testament that throw light on the subject of "eschatology" (the doctrine of last things). There are, to be sure, passages in the Old Testament which deal with eschatology. We may refer to a few of these in passing as they relate to New Testament eschatology, but our focus will be on the teachings of the New Testament. Neither will we examine closely every verse in the New Testament which has any allusion to eschatology. We will attempt to make a careful exegesis of all the major passages that treat the subject of eschatology.

This study will be divided into four main sections, each one exploring the teachings of a certain New Testament author. We shall begin with the teachings of Jesus as revealed in the Gospel records. These passages will serve as the basic and primary sources from which we arrive at our concepts of eschatology. After this we will proceed to examine the eschatological teachings of Paul, Peter, and John.

Where apparent contradictions appear our interpretations must be given in the light of Jesus' teachings. Actually, the eschatological teachings of all four men fit together in a beautiful symmetry. Concerning some of the details we cannot be certain, but the overall picture is clear and complete.

We must approach our study with an open mind, not prejudiced by preconceived notions. We have honestly tried to do exactly that. It is almost impossible, I suppose, to approach any subject without being influenced to some degree by preconceived ideas that have been injected into our minds, but as nearly as possible we have sought to approach this study with an open mind. We invite the reader to do the same.

C. E. Colton

Part I
The Eschatology of Jesus

1
THE END OF THE WORLD

There are a few veiled references to last things scattered throughout the teachings of Jesus as recorded in the four Gospels. However, the primary passage dealing with this subject as taught by Jesus appears in chapters 24 and 25 of Matthew's Gospel. Shorter versions of it appear in Mark 13 and Luke 21. In order to understand the eschatology of Jesus we need to concentrate on this passage.

It was Tuesday afternoon after a busy morning of conflict and controversy with the scribes and Pharisees that Jesus sat on the Mount of Olives with His disciples. The scene overlooked the city and the temple from which they had just emerged. En route from the temple, some of the disciples had remarked to Jesus about the vast and beautiful building of the temple area. This gave Jesus all the opening He needed for His discourse on coming events.

To their remark Jesus replied, "See ye not all these things? Verily, I say unto you, there shall not be left here one stone upon another, that shall not be thrown down." This started them to thinking about the future, and when they had crossed over the Brook Kidron and had found a place to sit down on the hill called the Mount of Olives, opposite Jerusalem, they requested of Jesus further information on this projected subject of future events. With this as a starting point, Jesus entered into a rather lengthy discourse in which He raised the curtain hiding the future from our view and gave us an insight, at least in general, of events that will come to pass at the "end of the age."

In summarizing this whole passage, we seem to come up with five general areas of thought in relation to last things: (1) the end of this world is coming; (2) tribulations are coming; (3) false Christs are coming; (4) Christ is coming; and (5) a final judgment is coming. In this chapter we shall concern ourselves with the first of these. The others will follow in the order named.

Concerning the end of the world, four questions cry out for an answer: what, how, when, and why? We find the answers in the words of Jesus in this discourse.

What

When we speak of the end of this world we are thinking of it as a material entity. Jesus seems to indicate in these verses that the world as a material substance will come to an end in complete destruction. But before we can confirm this postulate, we must do some analyzing and examining. Many commentators interpret the words of Jesus in these two chapters as referring to the destruction of the temple at Jerusalem rather than the destruction of the whole world. They see in this a clear-cut prophecy of the destruction of the temple in 70 A.D. by the Romans under Titus. We must admit that any interpretation followed will encounter difficult problems, but the one which seems, to me, to be least objectionable is that which interprets the entire passage as pointing to the final consummation of all things at the end of the age.

We must *disagree* with a number of very able Bible scholars, such as Bruce,[1] Broadus,[2] Morgan,[3] Lenski,[4] Criswell,[5] Summers,[6] et al., in our contention that Jesus had in mind the final consummation all through this discourse. In proof of this position, I point out several facts. In the first place, when Jesus said, "See ye not all these things? Verily I say unto you, there shall not be left here one stone upon another, that shall not be thrown down," it is not at all certain that he was speaking of the temple when some of his disciples remarked about the large and elaborate building with the large stones (some, we are told, were as long as eighty-five feet), but could it not have been that they were thinking of stones and buildings as such, rather than this particular temple?

They referred to the stones of the temple simply because they happened to be near it at the time. Their concern was not with the temple, as such, but with the idea of buildings and material constructions of this earth. They marveled at the largeness of the stones and, as Luke put it, at the beauty of the stones. In response to their concept of the beauty and permanence of earthly buildings Jesus said, "There shall not be left here one stone upon another." If He had meant it as a prediction of the fall of Jerusalem and the temple, it would hardly be accurate since some of the stones, as in the Wailing Wall, are still standing as they were—one upon another.

In the second place, it is difficult to reconcile the idea of the destruction of the temple in 70 A.D. with the coming of Christ and the end of the world. When the disciples sought further information on this first statement concerning the stones being thrown down, they phrased their question in this form: "Tell us, when shall these things be? And what shall be the sign of thy coming, and of the end of the world?

Whatever this destruction was, the disciples seemed to associate it with the return of Christ and the end of the world. If they were wrong, Jesus did not attempt to correct them. Some commentators have insisted that there are either two or three distinct questions here which have no direct relation to one another. (1) When shall these things be? (2) What shall be the sign of thy coming? and (3) What shall be the sign of the end of the world? Some lump the last two together, but most commentators definitely separate the first from the other two. But such an interpretation strains the natural and normal meaning and position of the three questions that are uttered almost in the same breath.

The explanation of Dr. Broadus[7] that the destruction of the temple was — in a sense — "a coming" of Christ and a consummation of an age, is wholly unsatisfactory. It is preposterous to think of it in any sense as a second coming of Christ and it is almost as unthinkable to associate it with any kind of a consummation of an era or age. We are willing to admit that the term, "the end of the world," is sometimes used to refer to the close of one era, but in most cases it clearly refers to the final consummation of all things. In the light of the context we can think of it as referring to nothing else. The year 70 A.D. could not be thought of as the closing out of any era.

In the third place, all through this predictive picture there are verses that speak unquestionably of the final end of the world. It would hardly be consistent to think of one verse as referring to the destruction of the temple and the next verse to the final consummation of the world, jumping back and forth throughout the passage in such a manner as one would desire. The overall picture is definitely one which is permeated with the thought of the final consummation of the world. I am inclined to believe, therefore, that everything in the passage has some connection or relation to the final end of all things.

Some commentators are willing to admit that in His discussion Jesus finally got around to the end of all things, but only after beginning with references to the fall of Jerusalem in 70 A.D.—but this position does not satisfy the clear language of the text, and those who hold it are at a loss to determine where one ends and the other begins. They insist that verse 34—"Verily I say unto you, This generation shall not pass, till all those things be fulfilled"—definitely refers to the destruction of the temple in 70 A.D., but they also admit that the verses immediately preceding refer to the end of the age. Thus do they find themselves hung on the horns of a dilemma. We insist that from the beginning Jesus was thinking in terms of the final consummation of this world.

This position is not without its problems. Our most serious difficulty confronts us in that 34th verse — "This generation shall not pass, till all these things be fulfilled." It is on the basis of this verse that most commentators insist that the destruction spoken of is the destruction of the temple in 70 A.D. If there were not other complications, I would gladly accept this rendering of these words. Since there are so many other elements which point in the other direction, I invariably find myself wondering if there is not another sense in which these words have been used.

We do not have to look long to find the clue for a different interpretation. That clue lies in the use of the word "generation." Most commentators have merely assumed that this word must refer to the people who were then living. In that sense these matters must come to pass before they die (or at least before all of them die). It is possible that some of the people living at the time Jesus uttered these words would still be living when Jerusalem fell in 70 A.D.

But this word, "generation," does not always carry this connotation. As found in the Septuagint, it is often used in the sense of a "kind" of man, rather than a contemporary man. The psalmist said, "Thou shalt preserve them from this generation forever" (Ps. 12:7). It is clear that the psalmist did not have in mind contemporary men but "evil" men. He also spoke of the generation of the righteous (Ps. 124:6; 73:15, etc.). Further examples may be found in Acts 2:4; Philippians 2:15; and Hebrews 3:10. Matthew and Mark both use this term in this sense. In Matthew 16:4 Jesus is reported as speaking of "a wicked and adulterous generation." For further examples see Matthew 17:17 and Mark 8:38. In the present connection the meaning of "this generation" is obviously a reference to the evil and rebellious people with whom Jesus and the disciples had been dealing all the day. The import of this statement, therefore, is as follows: Evil and godless people will not cease to exist on the face of this earth until all these events come to pass. With this meaning the context makes far better sense.

There is one more difficulty we must attempt to explain. That problem concerns the specific reference to the city of Jerusalem in Luke 21:20— "And when ye shall see Jerusalem compassed with armies, then know that the desolation thereof is nigh." Since Jerusalem is specifically named, most commentators have taken the position that He must have been referring to the encompassing of Jerusalem by the Roman soldiers in 70 A.D., and that the "abomination of desolation" must be the contamination of the temple by the Roman soldiers.

But this explanation does not satisfy the words of our text. Everything in the description of this destruction points to a final and complete destruction which would hardly be appropriate when applied to the siege of Jerusalem and the wrecking of the temple in 70 A.D. While the Roman soldiers wrought severe havoc upon the once-thriving city, it was *not* a final destruction. There is still a city of Jerusalem with several thousand inhabitants. There is even a temple there, even though it is a Mohammedan mosque.

The only destruction that could fit the description Jesus gives is one that looks to the end of all things. Jesus names Jerusalem in this description of final destruction of the world because this is where they happened to be at the time. Were Jesus living and speaking in New York City in this present day, would He not speak of the destruction of the World Trade towers in connection with His description of the end of the world? The specific reference to Jerusalem, a city with which they were familiar, made the idea of destruction all the more personal and real. If I were talking to a congregation of people in Dallas, Texas, about the final destruction of this material universe, I would describe it in terms of the destruction of the stately buildings of Dallas with which they were familiar. The end of the world, so far as His disciples were concerned, was the downfall of Jerusalem and all that with which they were familiar.

From this we conclude that Jesus was trying to tell His disciples and us that this world, in the sense of a material universe, will not continue in existence forever. It will come to an end, and even what we consider most permanent will crumble into dust when God brings all things to their final consummation.

How

Realizing that this world will come to an end, we next ask, How will this come to pass? How will it be destroyed? The answer to this question is not spelled out in this discourse. Peter gives us more detail of it in his Second Epistle, which we shall examine in a forthcoming chapter. There are some pivotal implications in the words of Jesus in this discourse. There are many instruments at God's command with which He could bring this world to naught. Three instruments seem to be implied in these verses. One is human strife and warfare. He speaks of nation rising against nation and kingdom against kingdom. Could it be that God will use the instruments of human warfare as one means of destroying this universe, either in whole or in part? Will we generate and use enough power in our fast-developing program of nuclear warfare to consume literally this world in which we live? There is this possibility, and if it is so done, it will only be in keeping with the permission, decree, and eternal purposes of God.

Another instrument in God's hand is natural calamity. Jesus speaks of the coming in that last day of "famines, and pestilences, and earthquakes in diverse places." Vast areas have been pulverized by such natural calamities. Could not God use such forces in nature to bring to pass His destruction of this world? Or He might use a more direct method, employing the services of a million heavenly angelic messengers to wreak vengeance on this material world. We know that He will use such heavenly messengers to gather together His redeemed from the four winds. With one swoop of His mighty hand, God could make powder out of this world and all that is on it. Just how He will do it we cannot say, but it would seem that He will put into use all of these instruments of destruction for the accomplishment of His purpose.

When

This is the question we are always asking; it is the question men have always been asking. The disciples asked Jesus, "Tell us, when shall these things be?" Jesus did not give a categorical answer, but He did give a few abstruse clues. He referred to several things that might be interpreted as signs of the approach of the end. The exact day or hour of the end Jesus does not say. In fact, He states that He Himself does not know, "But of that day and hour knoweth no man, no, not the angels of heaven, but my Father only" (Matthew 24:36).

Only the Father knows. Some of these signs are: a great tribulation, false Christs, and general turmoil. If these are signs, then we can truthfully declare that the end is not far away. We are on fairly good footing when we state that the end of this world is near, but we are completely out of bounds if we attempt to set up dates and schedules. There is no question about it—the end is near, but we must remember that this term, "near," is relative. It could mean today, tomorrow, or a thousand years from now, for a thousand years is but a moment when compared to eternity.

Surely Jesus would have us live every day in the expectancy of the end of this world. Whatever else we might learn from this passage is that every Christian should live every day in the consciousness that the end of this world is near. It would be rank presumption on my part if I should predict the end of this world on June 10 of 1999, or some other date, but when I write that the end of this world is near, and that it could be today, I am within the bounds of Christ's undeniable teaching.

Why

In answering this last question we should look at it from two angles. First of all, we should recognize that the world is coming to an end because God never intended for it to be eternal. He created it for time and space. It was created as an expediency to be used as a means of carrying out His eternal purpose for man. When He has finished and fulfilled His purpose in and through it, it is doomed for destruction. When it shall have fulfilled its intended purpose, it will then have no more reason for existing. It is then that God will bring it to naught. This world was made for man and not man for the world. Man is eternal, but the world is ephemeral. When this world shall have come to its end, it will not be because it has lost its momentum and played out. Rather, it will be because God has finished His purpose for it and has deliberately closed out its existence in its present form.

In the second place, let us remember that this prophetic utterance by Jesus concerning the end of the world was given in order that men might not place their hopes for eternity in it. Jesus wants us to know that this world will come to an end, and that if we lean too heavily on it there will come a day when we will have nothing on which to lean. The person who builds his life around the world and worldly things will one day wake up to the awful reality that the things on which he has anchored his life have disintegrated, and he is left sinking eternally into the bottomless pit. We must remember that the only things that endure are the things of the spirit.

If all we hold in our possession is what can be determined by worldly or earthly standards of measurement, then we are of all men most miserable—all these things will vanish and fade away into nothingness, leaving us empty. But the person who builds his life on spiritual realities and spiritual values will have something that will never decay or vanish away. The apostle John expressed it: "The world passeth away, and the lust thereof; but he that doeth the will of God abideth forever" (1 John 2:17). And Jesus makes it plain in this heart-to-heart talk with His disciples when He said, "Heaven and earth shall pass away, but my words shall not pass away" (Matthew 24:35).

2
THE GREAT TRIBULATION

A second event which comes in for consideration in the Olivet address of Jesus is a great period of tribulation. This great tribulation period is associated by Jesus with the end of the world and His return. According to Matthew's account we are told that "then shall be great tribulation, such as hath not been from the beginning of the world until now, no, nor ever shall be" (Matthew 24:21). In order to comprehend the significance of this statement we need to keep in mind all that Jesus said in this great eschatological discourse. References to the tribulation are interspersed all through it.

The Fact of a Future Tribulation Period for Christians

Whatever else Jesus may have intended to teach in this discourse He speaks clearly of a period of time when Christians will be subjected to a most rigorous ordeal of tribulation and suffering. Luke describes it like this: "But before all these things, they shall lay their hands on you, and shall persecute you, delivering you up to the synagogues and prisons, bringing you before kings and governors for my name's sake" (21:12).

There are three facts about this tribulation which must be recognized. First, it will be real and severe. The second fact to be noted is that these tribulations will come at some future time. The third fact is that these tribulations will come on the followers of Jesus. He is not describing here the plight of the wicked; it is clearly a reference to his own followers.

The Intensity of This Tribulation Period

Jesus uses two words in describing this tribulation which reveal something of the intensity of the tribulation. The first is the Greek word, *odis*, which carries the idea of pain as in childbirth. Only a mother knows the intensity of such pain. According to the testimony of many, there is no pain quite so severe. In fact, the original Greek word for "travail" was first coined with the idea of depicting the unique and intense suffering of a woman in childbirth. The other word is *thlipsis*, which carries the idea of bringing pressure to bear. It is highly significant in that it pictures one being crushed in a vice. It is a picture of pressure and oppression. When you put these words together you have a picture of intense suffering and pain. The period of tribulation will bring Christians into an experience of suffering the likes of which men have not known before. It will be no simple "headache" or "toe-ache"; it will be a major catastrophe.

The explanations given in the discourse clarify and corroborate the significance of the terms which we have just discussed. According to Matthew's account Jesus said, "Then shall they deliver you up unto tribulation, and shall kill you; and ye shall be hated of all the nations for my name's sake" (24:9). Mark is a little more vivid in the details of the description; "For they shall deliver you up to councils; and in synagogues shall ye be beaten; and before governors and kings shall ye stand for my sake, for a testimony unto them" (13:9).

The interesting fact about these sufferings is that they will not be the result of natural calamities, but of deliberate acts on the part of the adversaries of Christianity. The tribulations will be inflicted by people who are anti-Christian. Still more arresting is the fact that these adversaries of Christianity will include not only the avowed godless leaders of the state, but also the religious leaders of the day. And to the amazement of all, some of these persecutors will be of the same family with those who are persecuted.

Mark goes on to write, in reporting the words of Jesus on this subject, that "brother shall deliver up brother to death, and the father his child; and children shall rise up against parents, and cause them to be put to death" (13:12). The anguish and pain of the tribulations will be inflicted by those closest to the victims. This seems unbelievable, and yet already there are a number of instances in which this is actually being done. Reliable stories have come to us of mothers who have disowned and persecuted their own daughters because of their affiliation with Christ and Christians.

All in all, we can safely assert that the sufferings of the great tribulation will surpass anything that we have imagined.

The Time of This Tribulation Period

Again we ask with the disciples, "When shall these things be?" From where Christ sat on the Mount of Olives this period of travail for Christians was something for the future. There can be no question about this, but is it still in the future from our point of view? There was a great period of tribulation for Christians shortly before the fall of the temple in A.D. 70. Toward the close of the first century during the reign of Domitian, there was a period of tribulation for Christians even more severe and widespread than the first one. Through the centuries there have been seasons of bitter persecution against Christians. At the same time we might point out that some Christians have had to suffer at the hands of persecutors in every generation, even in ours. At the present, though, there is comparatively little real suffering being felt by Christians because of their Christian faith, at least in the Western World.

G. C. Berkouwer may have a point when he suggests that we should not think of these signs as events to occur in the far-distant future in an "end time," but as events having continual and progressive fulfillment beginning from the time of their utterance by Jesus to His disciples. They were events that were pertinent to the apostles. For that reason Jesus could address His disciples personally concerning this period of tribulation, emphasizing the personal pronoun, "you." "*You* will hear of wars and rumors of wars; see that *you* are not alarmed," etc. Dr. Berkouwer's comment in this connection is worthy of careful consideration:

> Eschatological preaching cannot be divorced from this contemporaneity. The signs are too concrete to be interpreted as an explanation of catastrophes to take place in some remote "end time"; they appear on the horizon of the lives of the apostles . . . . The "signs" are treated within the context of the contemporary situation and contemporary attitudes; which is why Luke's reference to Jerusalem is not a symptom of de-eschatologizing, but a meaningful perspective that rids eschatology of any futurism.[1]

Of course, we must recognize that these signs will be intensified as we approach the end time.

Though Jesus may have included in His thinking some of these periods when Christians suffered because of wild and unrestricted persecutions, we cannot believe that any of these would completely fulfill the prophetic utterance concerning a time of great tribulation. Everything in the passage seems to point to a time closely associated with the end of time or the consummation of the age. It must have reference to a period of special suffering the likes of which we have not known to this hour just before the end of time and the return of our Lord. According to Matthew, Jesus explains that "immediately, after the tribulation of those days the sun shall he darkened, and the moon shall not give her light, and the stars shall fall from heaven and the powers of the heavens shall be shaken: and then shall appear the sign of the Son of man in heaven" (24:29-30).

The periods of tribulation which have been known to Christians may be foregleams of this final period of unsurpassed tribulations, but we cannot think of them as having fulfilled the prophecy in whole. In fact, it could be that these tribulation periods are a part of the *great tribulation* which is yet to be climaxed. If the tribulation is like a woman with birth pains, they will most likely come intermittently with increasing intensity until the climax is reached. In describing some of the calamities that shall befall this world in the consummation of the age, Jesus adds that "All these things are the beginning of travail."

Naturally there are two questions with reference to time: When will the tribulation begin and how long will it last? There is no doubt, according to the words of Jesus, that the great tribulation period will immediately precede the end of the world and the return of our Lord. But we cannot be so certain about the duration of this period. Some Bible interpreters, such as Scofield,[2] Larkin,[3] Talbot,[4] Pentecost,[5] Criswell,[6] and many others, insist that this is to be a period of a literal seven years preceding the return of Christ to set up his millennial kingdom. Actually there is absolutely nothing in this Olivet discourse that would even remotely intimate that this is to be a literal period of seven years. Nor is there a statement to this effect anywhere else in scripture. There are two veiled references to a seven-year period divided into two equal segments of three-and-one-half each, one in Daniel 9:27 and the other in Revelation 11:3. All Bible students will recognize that both of these books are highly figurative in nature. To claim that the sevens here are to be interpreted literally or that they refer to the same event spoken of by Jesus in this address is presumption and speculation.

By mixing up a conglomerate of scriptural references some Bible interpreters have come out with an elaborate, sophisticated, and minute table of events for this seven-year period.[7] We would not go so far as to argue that they are wrong, but at best we must state that they are highly speculative with shaky biblical basis. It is not impossible that we could now be in this tribulation period, resting in between the intermittent shocks of the tribulation. However, if we are, there is bound to come in the future a climax that will issue in a tribulation for Christians which has never been known before.

Some Bible students have labored long in trying to fit this tribulation period into a millennial program. There are differences of opinion as to whether it comes before or after the millennial period referred to in Revelation 20:1-4. Any such attempt would only bring us into the realm of pure conjecture. Jesus has nothing to say in this whole discourse concerning any kind of a millennium. In fact, the only reference in the Bible to a millennium is that which occurs in the highly figurative passage in Revelation 20:1-4, a passage which we will examine more closely in a subsequent chapter.

Trying to reconcile these two portions of scripture with a millennial theme would only confuse the issue. By making a literal interpretation of the Revelation passage we would have to say that the great tribulation period must follow the millennial reign of Christ on earth. If we take the simple words of Jesus in our text, we would also have to say that the great tribulation period must immediately precede the second coming of Christ. If the second coming of Christ issues in a millennial reign of Christ, then you have the impossible task of trying to reconcile these two positions.

In arriving at the true meaning of Jesus' words in our text, we would be on much safer ground if we would forget, at least for the time being, the reference to the millennium in Revelation. It is far better to stay with the simple words of Jesus in this Olivet Discourse. According to these words we can safely indicate that there will be a special season of severe tribulation and persecution for Christians just before the end of this world and the return of our Lord. This, of course, could take place in our generation.

The Christian's Attitude Toward the Tribulation

Far more important than our ability to establish an exact date for the period of tribulation is our attitude toward that tribulation, should it come in our time. Whether or not it occurs generally in our day, persecution will come to some of God's people in one way or another even in our time, and the advice of Jesus in this passage is applicable to any Christian under any tribulation. According to Jesus in this address, two things should characterize a Christian in his attitude toward persecution, whether in the great tribulation period or in the presence of an individual experience. These two things are *faith* and *patience.*

In the hour of tribulation the Christian must have faith to believe that Christ will see him through and will give to him precisely the words he needs for that particular hour of testing. Jesus addressed these words to His apostles, but they are intended for all of the disciples of Jesus of any age: "And when they lead you to judgment, and deliver you up, be not anxious beforehand what ye shall speak; but whatsoever shall be given you in that hour, that speak ye: for it is not ye that speak, but the Holy Ghost" (Mark 13:11). This advice is for Christians facing severe persecutions at the hands of adversaries and has no connection with the idea of the preparation of a sermon for delivery.

Some preachers, it seems, have taken this advice of Jesus to mean that the preacher should make no preparation for his messages but simply rely on the Holy Spirit for help when preaching. This is a sad misinterpretation of this text. Jesus was talking about the answer of a Christian when he stands before those who falsely accuse him and persecute him. In such an hour God will give exactly the word that is most expedient for that time. Some of the most powerful, influential, and far-reaching statements have come from the lips of Christians who stood before their persecutors.

Stephen is a classic example. It was surely the Holy Spirit that inspired him to say as he stood before those who stoned him to death, "Lord, lay not this sin to their charge." This expression was perhaps the strongest human factor leading to the conversion of the great apostle Paul. Others through the years have given to the world tremendous messages of challenge and comfort as they have stood before the faces of their persecutors, often in the hour of death. God will never leave his child without the right word in the time of crisis.

Neither will He leave him without the comfort and grace to see the trial through to victory. Even though it leads to death, there is victory beyond. Death for the child of God is not a defeat but a victory. That is why Jesus can charge His disciples to stand up and hold the line, even if it means death, for He knows there is victory and glory beyond. The great tribulation, whenever it does come, will not be too much for the Christians. God will see to it that they have sufficient grace to endure it. Neither will He allow this tribulation to take all of His witnesses out of the world.

He will even shorten these days lest every voice be snatched away in the tribulation. In speaking of these tribulation days Jesus explains that "except the Lord had shortened the days no flesh would have been saved: but for the elect's sake, whom he chose, he shortened the days" (Mark 13:20). The term "saved" here does not refer to soul salvation. Obviously it has reference to the flesh. He taught that the tribulation of these last days would be so horrible that it would swallow up all Christians and remove them from the world, but God would shorten the days so there would still be left a testimony on earth at the end of the period.

The Outcome of This Tribulation Period

God has a purpose in all things, and that purpose always includes the eternal good of His redeemed children. Even so will it be with this period of persecution. God has not planned such a period merely to make it miserable for His children. On the contrary, it is designed to add glory and eternal luster to their spiritual life. Those who patiently endure these tribulations will come through them to a new and glorious realization of their own spiritual heritage.

Luke wrote: "In your patience ye shall win your souls" (21:19). Actually, it is "in your patience ye shall possess your souls."

Jesus has just said that in this tribulation period some of you will be put to death but "not a hair of your head will perish." This last quotation must not be taken literally. What he means is that, even though you may die physically, in your spiritual being not a hair of your head will perish—that is, you will lose nothing spiritually during this tribulation, even though you may die as the result of it. In fact, He assures them that, through all of this suffering, they will come into the true possession of their own souls.

This period of tribulation will bring out the true mettle in those who call themselves Christians. It will determine whether or not one is a true Christian. Those who endure to the end are the ones who shall be saved, for by such endurance they give evidence and proof of a valid Christian faith. In that day when iniquity shall abound in persecution, many of those who once claimed they loved Christ will find their love growing cold because it was never genuine in the first place. But, on the contrary, those who genuinely love the Lord will hold true through the bitterest trials. These are the ones who shall be saved. It is not that some Christians will fall by the wayside in the face of persecution and, therefore, lose their salvation. Rather, it is that some so-called Christians will fall by the wayside during the tribulation because they never had any genuine Christian experience. This is the obvious connotation of these words of Jesus: "And because iniquity shall be multiplied, the love of many shall wax cold. But he that endureth to the end, the same shall be saved" (Matthew 24:12,13).

Let us conclude this particular part of our study by reiterating that the great tribulation, though it will be an excruciating experience for all Christians caught in it, will issue in a new day for all who love the Lord. It will bring into full view our glorious, returning Lord with a joy even greater than that of a mother who looks into the face of her long-looked-for son after the travail of birth pains. It will be a marvelous revelation in which the true child of God will be seen over against those who only pretended to be Christians. It will issue in the eternal day of God's presence in glory. Let us all rejoice and take courage, knowing that if tribulations come they are only the precursors of a better and more brilliant day.

3
THE APPEARANCE OF FALSE CHRISTS

A third event mentioned by Christ in his Olivet Discourse is the appearance of an increasing number of false Christs and false prophets. In studying any aspect of the future we must go cautiously and conservatively, for it is easy to drift off into speculative fancies. On the other hand, we must not neglect or become indifferent toward that portion of Jesus' teaching in which He Himself carries us into the future. In our last chapter we dealt with the great tribulation period. There is a natural connection between that discussion and this one, for the presence of false Christs and false prophets is at least, in part, a cause of the tribulation. However, this is not to claim that all persecution will come from the pseudo-religionists.

The Identity of the False Christs

Jesus warns His disciples in the very beginning of His discourse that "many shall come in my name, saying, I am the Christ" (Matthew 24:5). Later on He teaches "There shall arise false Christs" (Matthew 24:24). We must distinguish between a false Christ and the anti-Christ. The false Christ is not the anti-Christ. The anti-Christ is one who is openly and avowedly against Christ; however, the Greek word, *anti*, could carry the idea of "in place of" or "instead of." In such a case it would be similar in meaning to the false Christs, but the context would not permit this. The term, anti-Christ, is found only in John's Epistles, and the context in each instance indicates the idea of someone who stands over against or in opposition to Christ. Therefore, the false Christs mentioned by Jesus in this discourse are entirely different from the anti-Christ mentioned by John. In a later chapter we will discuss John's anti-Christ in relation to eschatology. There is nothing in this discourse which can be identified with the anti-Christ as described by John in this Epistle or with the "man of sin" spoken of by the apostle Paul in his Second Letter to the Thessalonians, unless there should be a veiled allusion to it by the use of the plural pronoun in Matthew 24:9— "Then shall they deliver you up to be afflicted, and shall kill you." Just as there are many false Christs so there are also many anti-Christs.

But the false Christ is not "against" Christ, at least openly. He is one who claims to be Christ, that is, the promised deliverer of the Old Testament prophets. The false Christs of whom Jesus spoke in this text were not men who considered themselves to be the Christ of the Old Testament as over against Jesus of Nazareth. These men recognized Jesus of Nazareth as the Christ of the Old Testament prophets, but they themselves claimed to be this same Jesus Christ come back in the flesh. A few years ago a man came to our city who claimed, according to his own spoken and written word, that "He was the Lord Jesus Christ come back to earth in the form of man." This man could be identified as one of these false Christs.

There were men before the days of Jesus in the flesh who laid claim to Messiahship. Some of these are referred to in Jewish history. Even during the days of Jesus and soon thereafter men appeared, claiming to be the Christ. Two such men were referred to by Gamaliel in addressing the Sanhedrin concerning Peter and John who had preached that Jesus was the Christ. One was Theudas, "boasting himself to be somebody; to whom a number of men, about four hundred, joined themselves; who was slain; and all as many as obeyed him, were scattered, and brought to nought" (Acts 5:36). The other was Judas of Galilee, who "drew away much people after him" (Acts 5:37).

These men were false Christs, but they claimed to be the Messiah and would deny that Jesus was the Messiah. But the false

Christs who shall infiltrate the earth just before the consummation of the age will identify themselves with both Jesus and the Christ, claiming to be Jesus the Christ returning to earth. Mr. Sun Myung Moon of this present era might very well be identified as one of these false Christs. He has publicly claimed for himself Messiahship.

With these false Christs will be the false prophets (Matthew 24:11). Jesus reminds His disciples that "many false prophets shall arise." These false prophets will not claim to be the Christ in themselves, but they will point men to these false Christs, or at least they will misrepresent the true Christ. The world will be full of them. These false Christs will find their strongest support in these false prophets.

The Influence of These False Christs

We are told in our text that these false Christs and false prophets will "lead many astray" (Matthew 24:6,11,24). Their influence will be tremendous among men. This influence will be enhanced by the fact that they will be able to perform many signs and wonders (Matthew 24:24). It is not difficult for wicked men to use certain "tricks of the trade," which will make it appear that they have supernatural power. This is sometimes done by psychological effects, sleight, ventriloquism, or other carefully laid deceptive plans.

Human nature in general is gullible to such manipulations. In the Revelation, John describes how the Roman commune was able to do "great wonders, so that he maketh fire come down from heaven on the earth in the sight of men . . . and he had power to give life unto the image of the beast, that the image of the beast should both speak and cause that as many as would not worship the image of the beast should be killed" (Rev. 13:13-15). It is not difficult for those who are gifted in the art of deception to perform deeds which appear to involve supernatural power. For this reason their influence will be tremendous. Many simple-minded people will be deceived by this show of supernatural power. All of these false Christs and false prophets will be proficient in these deceptive arts.

Because of this deception they will be able to attract many followers. In some cases the following will be fantastic. So terrific will be their power and influence that they will attempt, and almost succeed, in deceiving the true children of God, the elect. Jesus implies as much when he states, "For there shall arise false Christs, and false prophets, and shall shew great signs and wonders; so as to lead astray, if possible, even the elect" (Matthew 24:24). In that conditional clause, "if possible," there is the implication that even the elect will be, at least for the moment, fascinated by the demonstrations of these so-called Christs, but it also implies that God has thrown a protective wall around His own redeemed children so it is impossible to lead them completely astray. Were it not for this protective wall with which God has circled His people, these false Christs might find them an easy prey for their satanic-inspired designs.

If one is led off completely by one of these false Christs so that he becomes a devoted follower of that false Christ, this action is a sure indication that such a person was never a true child of God, even though he may have borne that name. This does not mean that Christians will not be affected to some extent by these pseudo-Christs, for they could be attracted to the extent that they may lose some of the joy and effectiveness of their own Christian testimony. But there is deep consolation in knowing that Satan cannot touch the life of God's child to destroy it. He may harm and tantalize it, but he cannot destroy it. The true child of God is safe in the hands of God, and no one is able to pluck him out of God's hand (John 10:28,29).

The Warning Against These False Christs

Some may wonder why there would need to be any warning against the false Christs and false prophets, if God has so guaranteed the security of His own. But we must not overlook the fact that a part of God's plan of protection is through repeated warning. It is not the only protection, but it is a part of His protective plan. That is why it is so meaningful. All through His ministry Jesus warned His disciples against the encroachment of pseudo-religionists. In His great Sermon on the Mount he warned, "Beware of false prophets, which come to you in sheep's clothing, but inwardly they are ravening wolves" (Matthew 7:15). Jesus begins His discourse on these "last things" by saying, "Take heed that no man lead you astray" (Matthew 24:4). Several times he repeats this warning in the course of His discussion. Then He reminds them that He has warned them before (Matthew 24:25). Nor is this warning peculiar to Jesus alone. Long before Jesus appeared on the scene in the flesh, God spoke to His people through Moses in a timely word of warning against false religious leaders (Deut. 13:1-3). Other such warnings can be found in the writings of Paul and John (Gal. 1:8 and 1 John 4:1). It is good that we be constantly reminded of the dangers of being led astray by those who pose as Christian prophets. This is one of the ways by which God protects His people from the strong and deceptive pull of a forceful but spurious Christian leader.

The Significance of the Presence of These False Christs

The presence of these false Christs, according to Jesus in this discourse, is one of the signs of the end time. Not only will there be tribulations but also increasing numbers of these false Christs and false prophets. Do we gather from this that we are approaching the end of time? There are evidences of false prophets in our day. There are also those who claim to be the Lord Jesus himself. But these have been present in every generation since the days of Jesus until now. All of these may be little foreshadows of that which shall take place at the end, but undoubtedly Jesus was thinking of a time yet future when there shall be a noticeable proliferation in the number of false Christs and in the intensity of their work. When this will be no one knows. There is enough of this work today to cause everyone of us to live in the expectancy of the end of time.

Even though their presence is an indication of an approaching consummation of the age, their announcements concerning the Christ and His return are recognizably in error. They will say "Here He is" or "There He is." Some will call men to the wilderness to see Him; and others will point to some inner chamber. All such pronouncements are contrary to the basic principles of the teachings of Jesus. When He comes again all will be able to see Him at once. No one will have to go to the wilderness or to the inner chamber. It will be like the lightning which flashes from the east and is seen all the way to the west (Matthew 24:27). No one will have to announce His coming. Everyone will see it for himself. The returning Christ cannot be localized, and all who are localized—that is, limited to one particular place at a time—even though they be called Christ or call themselves Christ, are false to the core.

In speaking of these pseudo-Christs and pseudo-prophets, Jesus applies an ancient proverb: "Wheresoever the carcase is, there will the eagles be gathered together" (Matthew 24:28). The proverb itself is one that had been familiar to the Jews for many centuries. It was referred to by the author of the Book of Job in the long ago (Job 39:30).

Jesus used this same proverb on an earlier occasion (Luke 17:37). The true significance of this proverb as used by Jesus here is not clear. It could have several different implications. There is no question but that it is related to the foregoing verses about the false Christs and the false prophets, and it must have been intended to throw more light on the general subject of false prophets.

We understand that the eagle, or, as we would call it, the vulture, will swoop down upon that which is dead, the carrion, and consume it, but it is much more difficult to understand what this represents when applied to some aspect of Christian truth. The idea of Calvin[1] that Christ is the carrion and the believers are the vultures is abhorrent. It would be equally abhorrent to say that believers are the carrion and Christ the vulture. Alexander Maclaren[2] makes the vulture the symbol of divine judgment which swoops down upon a rotting, dead society. This idea applied to the context could mean that God's judgment will fall upon these false prophets who proposed to be alive but were dead. All of these interpretations fail to satisfy the conditions of the context.

It would seem more natural and feasible to suppose that these false prophets and false Christs were the vultures who had appeared on the scene because the world had become so corrupt that it was practically dead. This interpretation would fit into the predominant idea of the whole discourse—that all of these things are signals of the destruction of the world and the end of time.

These vultures of pseudo-Christianity come in great numbers only when the condition of the world has become so corrupt that it carries the stench of death. Could we not apply this principle in saying that where Christianity is kept pure and vigorous these false prophets are less apt to make their appearance? On the other hand, where Christianity has become decadent there the vultures of false Christs and false prophets flock in vast numbers. Whether these vultures be few or many, let us keep in mind the warning of our Savior lest we be led astray, even if but for the moment, by these pseudo-Christian leaders.

4
THE RETURN OF CHRIST

In this whole eschatological discourse by Jesus the primary, central event is the return of Christ to this earth. There are other subjects, to be sure, but all of them have a significant relation to the coming of Christ. The end of the world is associated with the coming of Christ. One seems to involve the other. In almost the same breath the disciples had asked: "What shall be the sign of thy coming, and of the end of the world?" (Matthew 24:3). Jesus indicates in this discourse that the great tribulation and the appearance of false Christs are to be interpreted as precursors of His return to earth. Therefore, we have now come to the main event: the return of our Lord.

This subject is a much-discussed one that is associated with many fanciful ideas in reference to the future. Some Bible students have made it a battleground of controversy with the focal point being the millennium. In setting forth and defending certain millennial positions some have forsaken the bounds of reason and sane Bible interpretation to employ all sorts of far-out speculations which they propose to have received from the Bible. This they have done by putting upon certain figurative Bible terms such interpretations as fit into their own fantastic notions. We admit that there is much to be said about the second coming of Christ which will not be found in this particular study of Christ's Olivet address. Our discussion here will be limited to what Jesus said to His disciples on this third day of His passion week. Other aspects of the second coming will come in for consideration as we study other parts of the New Testament on this subject.

The Expectation of His Return

The reference of Jesus in this discourse to the coming or appearing of the Son of man implies two things. First, it implies that Jesus is this "Son of man" who is coming. Nowhere in this discourse does Jesus say He is coming again. He does say a number of times that "the Son of man" is coming. And nowhere does he say that He is this "Son of man." But the implication is very strong. Throughout His ministry He has used this term, "Son of man," in referring to Himself. By virtue of that common usage it must have been understood by His disciples that when He spoke of the "Son of man," He was speaking of Himself. There has never been a difficulty at this point. No Bible student has ever questioned this identity.

Second, it implies that He had previously spoken of His return. The subject of His return is introduced in such a way that it implies a familiarity with it on the part of His disciples. No reference is made to a "second" coming or even to a "return." In every case it is referred to as a "coming" or, more literally, an "appearing." Since He was already in their presence it must have referred to another and later coming—thus a second coming or return. The familiarity of the disciples with this idea of a "coming" would indicate that Jesus had previously made promises of such a coming, and indeed He had.

The triumphal entry into Jerusalem only three days before had symbolically foreshadowed such a coming. Then on this same day only hours before Jesus had closed His last public discourse with an outburst of passion concerning Jerusalem and its plight, closing with this significant, though veiled, prophecy of His return: "Ye shall not see me henceforth, till ye shall say, Blessed is he that cometh in the name of the Lord" (Matthew 23:39). These and other references had led the disciples to believe that Jesus would come again, bringing to a climax the work of His kingdom. What they did not know, of course, was that before this "coming" He would be killed, rise again from the dead, and ascend back to the Father.

They perhaps thought that He might depart to the wilderness for a few days and then return to Jerusalem in a blaze of power and glory, ushering in the consummation of the age. At any rate, they had reason to believe that Jesus would come again. So we also do. We have the word of Jesus Himself that He will return to this earth. We have not only the promises He made before this incident on the Mount of Olives, but we also have the later promises which were given after His resurrection and just before His ascension.

In the light of these promises the disciples looked with expectancy to this "appearing" of the Son of man. They asked with eager hearts, "What is the sign of thy coming?" They had every reason to expect a tremendous, triumphant "coming" of their Messiah. So also do we. We ought to look expectantly toward the return of our Lord. The subject of the second coming of Christ ought to be of keen interest to every child of God, not only from the standpoint of curiosity and speculation, but also from the standpoint of the sheer thrill to think about the return of our Lord in glory, so we can see Him as He really is. It is with such feeling of expectancy that we approach this study of the return of our Lord.

The Uncertain Time of His Return

What is most *certain* about the return of our Lord is that the time of His return is *uncertain*. The time is not uncertain so far as God is concerned. He knows exactly when He is coming. The time of His coming has been established from before the foundation of the earth. There is nothing uncertain with God. Every detail has been planned and purposed from eternity. Whenever He comes again it will be at the exact moment as purposed by God from the beginning.

But so far as we are concerned the time of His coming is most uncertain. This simply means that God has deemed it wise to withhold from us the knowledge of the time of His return. He has not even divulged this information to His angels, nor even to the Son. "But of that day and hour knoweth no man, no, not the angels which are in heaven, neither the Son, but the Father" (Mark 13:32). "The Son" in this verse has reference only to the incarnate Christ. The Son in heaven must know all that the Father knows, but in His incarnate state, He voluntarily gave up the independent exercise of some of His divine prerogatives. It was a self-limitation. This self-limitation cut him off, in his incarnate state, from certain areas of divine knowledge. Included in this would be the knowledge of the time of his return. For this reason He could truthfully say that not even the Son knows "of that day and that hour."

If the incarnate Son knew not the time of His own return to earth, how much less do we who are His followers? Any prediction naming time and date is based upon rank presumption and ignorance. This does not mean that we cannot know when the time is near, for Jesus said to His disciples, "Now learn a parable of the fig tree; when his branch is yet tender and putteth forth leaves, ye know that summer is nigh, so likewise ye, when ye shall see all these things, know that it is near, even at the doors" (Matthew 24:32,33). There is a vast difference between saying that a thing is near and that it will come to pass on such and such a day at such and such an hour. That term, "near," is relative and could mean anything from one moment to a thousand years or more. In this sense it is not wrong for us to announce to the world that the return of our Lord is nigh. In fact, there is enough evidence of the presence of the things described by Jesus in this discourse to merit the conclusion that the end is near and that the coming of the Lord "draweth nigh."

In another parabolic statement Jesus speaks of His coming as the coming of a "thief in the night" (Matthew 24:43). This does not mean that Jesus is like a thief, except in one aspect—no one knows when He is coming. A thief would never be successful in his work if his victims knew when he was coming, for that is one thing no one knows but the thief himself. The secret of his success is in the element of surprise.

So also will the return of our Lord be. He will come at a time when we least expect Him. In another parable Jesus likens His coming to the return of a householder who had left his business in the hands of servants. One servant performed his duty faithfully, but the other one, thinking that his lord would not return for some time, neglected his responsibility for his own selfish designs. But concerning this evil servant, Jesus said that "the lord of that servant shall come in a day when he looketh not for him, and in an hour that he is not aware of" (Matthew 24:50).

The Universal Visibility of His Return

When Christ does come, whether "at even, or at midnight, or at the cockcrowing, or in the morning" (Mark 13:35), he will be seen by all at once. "For as the lightning cometh out of the east, and shineth even unto the west; so shall also the coming of the Son of man be" (Matthew 24:27). In likening His coming to the lightning, Jesus was not thinking of its brilliance, its power, or its form. The context indicates that He was thinking of it from the standpoint of its visibility to all men, from the east even to the west.

This is in contrast to those false prophets who say that He is here or He is there. He will not be localized anywhere. He will be seen by all simultaneously. Some will object, saying that this is impossible since some people live on opposite sides of this global earth. But this objection holds no problem to those who believe in the supernatural, miraculous power of this returning Christ. The miracle of His return will be in full view of every creature who lives upon this earth. Every eye shall see him in that moment. No one will have to say "come and see."

The Glory of His Return

Even though we do not know many of the details of His coming, we do know that He will come in splendor. It will be quite a contrast to His first coming. The first time He came in humility, being born in a manger, unnoticed and unheralded by the world at large. But when He comes again it will be in dazzling glory and unsurpassed splendor.

According to Matthew, Jesus describes it like this: "And then shall appear the sign of the Son of man in heaven: and then shall all the tribes of the earth mourn, and they shall see the Son of man coming in clouds of heaven with power and great glory. And he shall send his angels with a great sound of a trumpet and they shall gather together his elect from the four winds, from one end of heaven to the other" (Matthew 24:30-31). In His first advent He was rejected and despised by men, "a man of sorrows and acquainted with grief," but when He comes the second time every knee will bow before Him and all people shall see Him in all of his glory and power. No one will question His deity or authority. These things will be so obvious that everywhere there will be only fear, awe, and adoration.

The Preparation for His Return

The burden of this whole discourse is wrapped up in the idea of preparation. The whole message was designed to help His disciples prepare for His coming. If our Lord is to return in such resplendent glory, we, as His followers, should give some thought to our preparation for such a return. But how shall we prepare for His coming? There is much more to it than an experience of faith in which we accept Christ as Savior. In fact, this discourse is addressed to believers, not unbelievers. Jesus is not talking about preparation for the life to come by reception of Him as Savior and Lord. In other places He does have much to say on this aspect of it, but in this particular discourse He is thinking of the preparation Christians ought to make for His return, to the end that they might share in the glory of it. A man may be a Christian and still be totally unprepared for the return of His Lord, unprepared in the sense that He is in no position to receive with joy and delight the glorious appearing of his Savior.

Jesus has three things to say about our preparation for His coming. These three things may be summed up in three words: *watch*, *pray*, and *work*. If we are to participate in the glory of His coming we must watch for that coming. If He comes when we are not expecting, it will take us so long to get over the shock and surprise of it, that we will miss the glory of it. This does not mean that we should stand literally gazing into heaven twenty-four hours a day. This, of course, would be impossible.

Paul had to rebuke and correct the Christians of Thessalonica for putting such an interpretation on His message concerning the second coming of Christ. Nor does it mean that we must talk constantly of His coming, with nothing else ever entering our minds. The symbolism found in the parable of the ten virgins suggests that they did no wrong in going to sleep. It was natural for them to sleep, but they went to sleep with the consciousness of the possible coming of the bridegroom. To watch, as implied by Jesus in this discourse, is to live in the consciousness of His coming at all hours of the day and night. Of course, this does not mean that one may not do or think about other things. To be sure, it will be necessary for him to do many other things, but all the while there should be present in his subconscious mind the thought of the Savior's possible return at any moment.

Even while one sleeps there ought to be present the thought of the Lord's return in that subconscious mind. Did you ever go to sleep at night with a keen sense of your having to get up at a certain early hour? Even though you slept there was your subconscious feeling that never departed from you, and because of this the faintest whisper would arouse you. Even so should the subconscious feeling of the imminent return of our Lord possess our minds even while we sleep. In this sense Jesus urged His disciples to "take ye heed, watch and pray: for ye know not when the time is. . . . Watch ye therefore: for ye know not when the master of the house cometh, at even, or at midnight, or at the cockcrowing, or in the morning: lest coming suddenly he find you sleeping. And what I say unto you I say unto all, watch" (Mark 13:33,35-37).

The second preparatory exercise is prayer. Prayer is communion with God through His Son. If we are to be ready for His return, we must keep in constant touch with Him through prayer. Prayer brings us into the realization of His presence. There is a reality and sweetness about His presence in prayer, but it is nothing compared to His presence as we shall feel it and see it at His coming. However, if we have kept in touch with Him through prayer, the transition from a spiritual presence to a bodily presence will not be so shocking. Those who have experienced His abiding presence in a life of unceasing prayer will be in a much better position to appropriate the glory of His bodily presence at the *parousia*.

The third element of our preparation for His coming is work. If we would be ready to share in the glory of His return, we must be found working at the job He has given us. This is most forcefully illustrated in the parable of the householder who left a responsibility to his servants while he went away on a long journey. They were to serve by giving meat to those who lived in the house in due season. Then Jesus added this beatitude: "Blessed is that servant, whom his lord when he cometh shall find so doing" (Matthew 24:46). The best thing that could happen to that servant, so far as his lord was concerned, was to be found doing the work to which he had been assigned when his lord returned.

While we watch and while we pray, we must be busy at the task assigned to us by our Lord. What is that task? It is to take the gospel of salvation in Christ to all the world. The Christian who is not busy at this task when His Lord returns will find His coming most embarrassing. The best preparation that you can make for the second coming of Christ is to give complete devotion to the task of world missions. Blessed is that Christian whom his Lord when He comes shall find working faithfully at the task of sharing Christ with the world, through giving of his means to support the mission program of his church, prayer, and personal testimony.

5
THE FINAL JUDGMENT

In chapter 24 of Matthew's Gospel, Jesus seems to tell us of His return to earth and of the events leading up to it. The 25th chapter describes the final judgment which issues out of His return to earth. It cannot be denied that we have here a picture of judgment. It is portrayed in three scenes, two parables, and a prophetic account of the judgment built around metaphoric terminology. We cannot be dogmatic about the details, but everything seems to point to a final judgment as a consummation of the whole program of redemption in which the redeemed will be properly rewarded and the unregenerate consigned to eternal torment. There may be other aspects of the final judgment which are revealed in other scripture passages. These will be considered in later chapters of this study, but here we are thinking only of those aspects of the final judgment which are revealed in this particular eschatological discourse of Jesus.

The Administrator of the Judgment

We need not linger long on this first point, for it is quite clear in our text that Jesus Himself will be the executor of this final judgment. In the two parables the administrator of the judgment is not identified, but in the last picture we are told: "When the Son of man shall come in his glory, and all the holy angels with him, then shall he sit upon the throne of his glory; and before him shall be gathered all nations: and he shall separate them one from another" (Matthew 25:31-32). The one who now serves as our Savior and Redeemer will then serve as our Judge. True, God is the great Judge of all, but the Father "hath committed all judgment unto the Son" (John 5:22). This also corresponds with John's apocalyptic picture from the Isle of Patmos in which the Son, the Lamb, takes the book of judgment out of the hand of Him who sits on the throne and prepares to execute the judgments written therein. Jesus is now the long suffering Savior, full of mercy and grace, but then He will become the stern Judge to administer judgment without compromise.

The Subjects of the Judgment

Who are these who shall stand before Jesus as their Judge in that final day? The answer to this question is not so easy. There have been widely varying views at this point. Perhaps the most common view is that which looks upon the first and the last scene (the ten virgins and the sheep and goats) as depicting a general judgment to which all people—past, present, and future—will be involved. The second scene concerning the talents is usually applied as a judgment upon Christians. Through the years I have taken just such a position, but upon a more careful examination of this whole passage I have been led to pursue a different view. There are many different variations of thought concerning the subjects of this judgment.

One interesting theory is that of Plumptre[1] who has concluded that the parable of the virgins refers to all Christians; that of the talents to those that hold any office or ministry in the church; and the last picture, to the heathen. It is doubtful that Jesus had any such distinctions as this in mind. Dr. G. Campbell Morgan[2] has divided the whole Discourse (chapters 24 and 25) into three main parts. The first part (24:1-35) deals only with Israel after the flesh; the second (24:36-25:30) refers to spiritual Israel or the church; the last (25:31-46) treats the Gentile nations or the heathen.

According to this arrangement, the two parables would refer to Christians and the last picture to the heathen. This view also seems to impose distinctions that are not clearly revealed in the text. Meyer and others understand this judgment as referring to Christians only, but this is highly improbable in view of the

"Christians" on the left who are told to "depart from me, ye cursed, into the eternal fire."

We must admit there are some serious problems in arriving at the identity of these people who shall thus be judged. According to this initial presentation, it would appear that in each scene Jesus has in mind His own followers, or Christians. All ten of the virgins are presented to us as equally looking forward to the coming of the bridegroom. The talents were given by the Lord to "his own servants." And the sheep and goats of the third scene are both taken from the flock of the shepherd, and He will separate them "as a shepherd divideth his sheep from the goats."

Looking at it from the point of view of the consequences it appears that He has in mind not only His own followers but avowed disbelievers as well. In the case of the virgins the five unprepared ones are left outside, and the door is shut against them. The one-talent servant who hid his talent is cast into outer darkness, where there is weeping and gnashing of teeth. And in the last scene the goats are told to "depart from me, ye cursed, into everlasting fire, prepared for the devil and his angels" (Matthew 25:41).

How can we reconcile these two aspects of our threefold picture? In all three of these scenes it is difficult to get away from the impression that Jesus is speaking of certain aspects of the final judgment following immediately upon His return to earth. All three seem to bear upon the same general theme. There is no good reason for supposing that He has completely changed from one scene to another the original subjects of this final judgment.

It occurs to me that Jesus is speaking of all those who profess to be His followers, those who consider themselves to be in the ranks of Christians. He is showing how in the final day the true shall be separated from the false in religion. This position is in keeping with the tone of His message all the way through this discourse. All day long He had been thinking and talking in terms of religious pretenders. He had bitterly denounced the hypocrisy of the scribes and Pharisees. He had spoken frequently in this discourse about false Christs and false prophets. It is this idea that He seems to have in mind as He continues to draw the picture of these coming events issuing in a final judgment that shall bring all things into their proper light. Men may pose as religious leaders, but in the final judgment their hypocrisy and pretense will be exposed openly and justifiable condemnation administered.

This position, I realize, is not without its problems. For instance, there is the reference to "all nations" who shall stand before Him. However, this could very easily have reference to the fact that men from all nations will be present at this judgment. The expression is so used on other occasions. Someone else may ask, "But what about those who make no profession of religion? Will they not also be judged in this last day?" There is no doubt but that they will, and there are many other scriptures to verify this fact, but in this particular passage Jesus seems to have in mind the professing Christians. It is not that the others will not be judged, but simply that at this particular time He is concentrating with His disciples on the judgment of those who call themselves Christian or religious. If he had been speaking of all men generally, it is hardly probable that He would have based His judgment upon giving a cup of cold water to a little one. This we shall explain further in a subsequent paragraph. In all three pictures, therefore, it seems that those who stand before the Judge to be judged are people who consider themselves followers of Jesus or at least religious.

The Nature of the Judgment

Judgment naturally divides itself into two parts. It involves first the rewarding of those who have given evidence of genuineness. Some of those who stand before the Lord in that day will be put to the test and found genuine. These will be properly rewarded with life and joy. This aspect of the judgment is described by Jesus in these three pictures. The five wise virgins represent genuine Christians. They are privileged to enter into the wedding chamber and participate in the joys of the wedding festivities. It is a picture of delight and happiness. Those who are truly ready at His coming will be given entrance into the wedding chapel of heaven, where they shall behold the magnificent occasion of the wedding of the Son of God in all of His splendor and glory to the Bride, His Church, the redeemed in all of their blood-washed purity.

The second scene describes the rewards which shall be bestowed on the redeemed for faithful service in the use of the talents which have been given. These rewards will not all be identical, for the capacities and talents will be different, but each one will be given all of the reward which he is able to receive in the light of his capacity.

The third scene describes the eternal blessedness of the genuinely saved. The judge shall say to these: "Come, ye blessed of my Father, inherit the kingdom prepared for you from the foundation of the world" (Matthew 25:34). The reward of the redeemed is entrance into a glorious kingdom with full access to every benefit of it. These are pictures to delight the soul.

But as we turn to the other side of the judgment, it is a picture of darkness, suffering, and despair. For those who are false followers of the Christ, this final judgment will be far from pleasing. It will be the occasion for deep distress and anguish. Again we have three pictures. In the first we see the five foolish virgins being left on the outside with the door forever shut. They had come to knock on the door but found it shut. To be left on the outside knowing that the door will never open again is to experience a panicky sense of distress and remorse.

Our second picture reveals a servant who is cast "into outer darkness," where there will be weeping and gnashing of teeth. Here is a picture of fearfulness, pain, and torment. The last scene leaves us with a portrait of horror. To those on His left Jesus says, "Depart from me, ye cursed, into everlasting fire, prepared for the devil and his angels." To be forever burning but never burned up will be the lot of those who stand before the Judge unprepared, even though they may bear the name Christian. The judge will be able to see through their camouflage and hypocrisy and will consign them to the torments of hell, according to the measure of true justice.

We cannot agree with Dr. G. Campbell Morgan's position that the judgment spoken of here is a judgment of nations as such. It is his opinion that Jesus will summon the nations before him to determine their Christian character. Those found wanting in Christian character will be doomed; the others will be given a place of leadership in his millennial kingdom on earth. His explanation is as follows:

> The Son of man is the Administrator of the affairs of the earthly kingdom, and this is His picture of the initial process in the consummation of that administration—the gathering of the nations, the separating between them, the finding of a verdict, and the passing of a sentence. . . . This is the national separation. He first gathers the nations into one, so breaking all our present divisions and separations. But then He makes a new separation. . . . The king is seen establishing the earthly kingdom, and He calls righteous people to inherit it. . . . That is to say, nations will be admitted to the inheritance of the kingdom upon the basis of their attitude toward Christ as revealed in their attitude toward his people during the preliminary period. . . . Only remember that here Christ is not dealing with the subject of the soul's destiny either in heaven or in hell. They are terms that have to do wholly with the setting up of the kingdom here in this world, and those methods by which he will assume the reigns of government, excluding some and including others.[3]

All of this seems rather far-fetched. I would have to stretch my imagination beyond all sense of reason to see this in the words of our text. The only connection I can see between this interpretation and the text is the reference to "all nations," but this expression is commonly used in reference to people of all nations or all people. If this is a destiny of nations as such in this world, what is the significance of the term "everlasting fire?" Let us come back to emphasize, as we see it, here is a picture of the final destiny of all those who pose as followers of Jesus, both genuine and the spurious.

The Basis of the Judgment

On what basis are some judged worthy of eternal bliss and others judged worthy of eternal torment? The answer to this question will be most difficult to reconcile with the total teaching of Jesus unless we take the position that all of those who stand before this throne of Jesus are professed followers of Jesus. In this particular case He is not judging between the Christian and the one who openly opposes Christianity; rather, He is judging between the true Christian and the spurious Christian. In such a situation he shows us how He determines which ones are sheep and which ones are goats. This is determined by what they do. We are not saved by the doing of certain deeds, but the genuineness of our profession is determined by what we do or leave undone. The basis, therefore, of this judgment is the conduct of the individual. Let us look at it a moment in each of our three pictures.

In the case of the virgins, all ten of them were waiting for and wanted to have a part in the coming of the Bridegroom to His wedding. They were all on the same side, at least on the surface, but five of them were wise and were granted the privilege of entering in for the wedding. Five of them were foolish and were forbidden entrance. We usually hear that they did not get in because they had no oil in their lamps. The oil in this case would become the symbol of saving grace. But actually, on closer investigation, it will be noticed that they were forbidden entrance, not on the basis of their having no oil, but on the basis of their lateness.

There is nothing in the parable to indicate that they could not have gone in with the others, even though they may have been a little embarrassed by their lack of light in their lamps. In no other parable is it so easy to drift into all kinds of allegorical interpretations, and many have succumbed to this tendency. But let us try to see the principles of the lesson which Jesus sought to teach by this parable.

Dr. A. B. Bruce has an excellent treatment of this parable in his *The Parabolic Teaching of Christ*, in which he points out that "the essential element is the welcoming of the bridegroom; the carrying of lights is an accident due to the fact that the procession takes place by night."[4] He goes on to show that the folly of the foolish virgins was in insisting on going out of their way to find an accessory to the main emphasis. Their fault was in putting so much emphasis on the superficial aspects of the event that they missed the main event. There are many so-called Christians in this category. They give so much concern to the incidental and superficial aspects of Christianity that they miss the main element of personal relationship to the Christ. These will be like the five foolish virgins of the parable; they will be left on the outside, even though they have diligently gone through many of the forms of Christianity. Surely Jesus must have had the Pharisees in mind when giving this parable.

In our second picture the one-talent man who refused to use his talent is cast into outer darkness. His being cast into outer darkness was not based on the fact that he had failed to use his talent. It would be contrary to everything else Jesus taught to say that a genuine Christian will be cast into hell if he does not use the talent God has given him, but it is reasonable and consistent to say that the man, even though he professes to be a Christian, who makes no attempt to use the talents God has granted, is giving evidence by that indifference that he was never a genuine follower of Jesus to begin with. Thus does Jesus determine between the genuine and the false among those who call themselves religious. It is not the case of a Christian losing his place in the kingdom, but it is the case of a spurious Christian who is brought into the true light of his real condition.

In the third picture men are turned into everlasting punishment because they did not minister to a suffering follower of Jesus. Dr. John A. Broadus, in *The American Commentary*, makes the following appropriate comment on this passage:

> It would be a grave mistake to suppose that nothing will be regarded in the judgment, nothing to help in determining a man's future, but the simple question whether he has been benevolent towards suffering Christians.... It is also a mistake to infer that only actions will enter into the judgment. The essence of the passage is that the actions in question will be accepted as indicating personal relation to Christ; and it is really personal relation to Christ, as acted out in the life, that will fix eternal destiny.[5]

No man's eternal destiny will be determined by his giving of a cup of cold water to a thirsty Christian, but when people who call themselves Christian stand before our Lord in the final judgment, the true will be divided from the false as evidenced in their concern for the needs of the true follower of Jesus. The giving of a cup of cold water will not save a man's soul, but it may be the evidence that one has already been saved. It is a personal relationship of faith in Christ that saves, but we prove that we have such faith by our conduct toward people, especially the followers of Jesus, in their needs. In this is the true significance of these precious words of Jesus, "Inasmuch as ye have done it unto one of the least of these my brethren, ye have done it unto me." In other words, "if you manifest a love toward the least of those who follow Me, it is an indication that you love Me." It is impossible to love Christ without manifesting it in our love for others. In this manner shall the Judge separate the sheep from the goats when He comes to sit upon His throne in judgment. We may fool men here some of the time, but if we are not genuine in our devotion to Christ, our hypocrisy will be brought into the full light of Christ's scrutinizing eye when we stand before Him at the final judgment.

6
ANOTHER PICTURE OF THE RETURN OF CHRIST

Just before He ascended back to His Father in heaven, Jesus had another encounter with His disciples in which the curtain was rolled back, revealing another look into the future. The disciples realized that the unusual events which had recently occurred must be harbingers pointing to the consummation of the kingdom of God. However, in spite of the teachings of Jesus, their concepts of the kingdom were still interpreted in terms of a political reign of Christ on earth. With this in mind they address a question to the resurrected Christ. "Lord, wilt thou at this time restore again the kingdom to Israel?" (Acts 1:6). They could not dismiss from their minds the idea that Jesus, the Messiah, would rescue the Jews from the Roman yoke and re-establish the nation of Israel, with Jesus Himself as their new king and prince.

But Jesus disillusioned their minds with this astonishing answer: "It is not for you to know the times or the seasons, which the Father hath put in His own power" (Acts 1:7). Then He reminded them of the promise of the Holy Spirit and of their commission to be witnesses to Him in Jerusalem, Judea, Samaria, and the whole world. Immediately following these words the disciples watched in astonishment as Jesus ascended into the clouds above. As they stood there gazing up into the clouds in which Jesus had disappeared, two angelic beings in white stood beside them with the following announcement: "Ye men of Galilee, why stand ye gazing up into heaven? This same Jesus, which is taken up from you into heaven, shall so come in like manner as ye have seen him go into heaven" (Acts 1:11). Thus are we privileged, along with the disciples, to witness another glimpse into the future. It concerns the major event of all eschatological considerations—the return of Christ to this earth.

This picture gives little, if anything, in addition to that which Jesus gave in His Olivet address. It does verify and amplify the picture which He gave on that occasion.

The Certainty of His Coming

The primary purpose of the angels in announcing the return of Jesus was not to describe the manner of His coming but the certainty of it. Whatever else may have been intended by these words from the two angelic beings, it is certain that their main objective was to impress upon the hearts of those disciples that He would as surely return as He went away. The comparison is not between the manner of His going away and the manner of His return but the fact of His going away and the fact of His return.

The most pertinent feature of the second coming of Christ is always the certainty of it, and this is where the emphasis ought always to be. Just as surely as He went away He will come again. The passing of the centuries may have a tendency to cause us to question the certainty of it, but those who believe the Bible will find in the delay only a fuller assurance of the fact of it. If I believe that Jesus came the first time nearly 2,000 years ago in real humanity, I must also believe that He will come the second time to this earth in person. If the men on Bataan could have confidence in the promise of MacArthur that he would return, how much more should we who believe in the deity of Jesus have absolute confidence in His promise announced through the angels to His disciples on this occasion?

The Manner of His Coming

While the primary objective of the words of this passage is to confirm the certainty of His return, incidentally it does reveal some features of the manner of His return. At least three things seem to be indicated as to the manner of His second coming.

First, we may gather from this passage that His return will be from above. If he "shall so come in like manner as ye have seen him go into heaven," He will doubtlessly return out of the clouds from above, for it was into them that He went. He will not come up out of the earth. He will come from above where He was seen going away.

Second, we may also conclude from this text that He will come in body. If He comes as He went away, He will come as a real human being. He will be no phantom. His bodily presence will be as real as was His bodily presence among the disciples before He ascended. Even though His resurrected body was somewhat different from His pre-resurrection body, it was nonetheless real and recognizable by His disciples. He is with us now in the person of the Holy Spirit, but then He will be with us in body. It will be a bodily, visible presence. We shall be able to see Him with our physical eyes, as well as our spiritual eyes.

Third, we may also surmise from this text that Jesus will return in glory. It was a glorious ascension which they had witnessed. Even so shall it be a glorious return that His redeemed shall witness one day. This also coincides with the picture Jesus gave His disciples on Mount Olivet: "When the Son of man shall come in his glory, and all the holy angels with him, then shall he sit upon the throne of his glory" (Matthew 25:31). The details of this glory are not clearly defined here, but the very tone of it suggests a glorious return. Here we learn only that as His going away was a glorious and impressive experience so will His return be. The glory of it will exceed our fondest dreams.

The Effect of the Promise of His Return

Jesus was far more concerned with the attitude of His disciples toward the promise of His return than He was with their understanding of all the details of that return. From this first chapter of The Acts of the Apostles, Christians should learn three lessons concerning their attitude toward the promise our Lord's return to this earth.

What's Next?

First, we should not stand starry-eyed, gazing into heaven looking for the appearance of our Lord. The disciples were standing in somewhat of a dazed condition looking into the cloud which had received their Lord, as if He might presently reappear out of that same cloud. The angels had to correct their false impressions by commanding them to return to the task which He had assigned them. The Christians at Thessalonica had this same trouble, and the apostle Paul had to correct them.

Few, if any, modern-day Christians have this problem. For the most part we have swung to the other extreme, giving little or no thought at all to the return of our Lord. Once in a great while we hear of someone who stands looking up into heaven for the appearing of Jesus. One woman, it was reported, went up on the highest hill she could find near her home and sat with her suitcase packed for several days, looking for the coming of Jesus.

Second, we should learn from this passage not to spend time and energy in speculative contemplation on the events associated with the second coming. Even though the majority of Christians are characterized by a regrettable apathy as to the second coming, there are many who have been sidetracked into giving the chief emphasis of their lives to speculative conjectures on the details of the events connected with the return of our Lord. And this is pathetic. What the angels said to these disciples who witnessed His ascension clearly indicates that there are other things more important than speculative studies on the details of the second coming. It is not our business to map out a detailed program of events for the Lord's return.

We are told very plainly in this first chapter that "it is not for you to know the times or the seasons, which the Father hath put in his own power." Human curiosity invariably seeks expression at this point. Some men have worked out elaborate schemes and schedules for the Lord's return. Some have gone so far as to make it a test of fellowship, and, in some cases, of salvation. To give some attention to matters of eschatology is indeed permissible and even wise. But to make such matters tests of fellowship and objects of pre-eminent concern is to misinterpret the scripture and the mind of Jesus.

Third, the only real Christ-like attitude toward the return of Jesus is that which inspires complete devotion to the commission which Christ has given to us. The best possible preparation which can be given for the second coming of Christ is an unreserved dedication to the task of world missions. The disciples responded to the message of the angels by returning to Jerusalem to wait for the power of the Spirit with which they would carry the gospel of Jesus to the whole world. This action is an interpretation of the words of the angels and an answer to the question, "Why stand ye gazing up into heaven?"

When we think of the Lord's return and of the possibility of its realization, immediately one thought should surge through our being and completely possess us in mind and soul. That thought should be: "Have I done all that Jesus wanted me to do? Have I been the witness that he commissioned me to be?" Such questions as these should take precedence over all others.

Jesus is coming again! But what does that mean to you? Is it a fantastic event which interests you only from the standpoint of what He will look like when He comes or what He will do and how He will do it? Or does it bring you into the consciousness that you will stand before Him to give account of the stewardship He left with you? Will you have to hang your head in shame when He asks if you have been faithful to the task He left with you? It is not a question of which cloud He will ride on or what type of clothes He will be wearing, or how many angels He will have with him. It is, rather, a question of will I be prepared to meet Him with the joy and peace of knowing that I have done my best in the task he had assigned me.

Part II
The Eschatology of Paul

7
THE CHRISTIAN DEAD AND THE SECOND COMING

In the writings of the apostle Paul there are many allusions to the second coming of Christ and the consummation of the age; however, there are only three major discussions related to eschatology: 1 Thessalonians 4:13-5:11; 2 Thessalonians 2:1-17; and 1 Corinthians 15:1-58. The first of these will be the basis of our study in this chapter.

When Paul was with the Thessalonians he must have talked much about the glorious return of our Lord to earth. He must have painted an impressive picture of a triumphant Lord coming in splendor to gather up His redeemed from the earth and to join with them in a glorious celebration of victory. This return Paul presented as something which was imminent, something that they could expect at any moment.

While they awaited this momentous day some of their Christian friends and loved ones had died. It is possible that some of these had died as martyrs in the cause of Christ. The death of these loved ones raised a question in the minds of these Thessalonian Christians which had not been anticipated either by Paul or by them when Paul was present with them. Would these deceased loved ones miss out on this wonderful occasion when the Lord would come back to earth in all of His glory? These Christians had been led to believe that the coming of the Lord would be witnessed only by those who were living on the earth at the time of His coming. This question disturbed them considerably. They had expressed their concern about this matter to Timothy when he was present with them and Timothy, in turn, passed the question on to Paul when he saw him in Corinth.

One of the reasons for writing this epistle was to answer this question which had arisen in the minds of the Christians of Thessalonica. Paul faced the problem very frankly and gave a satisfactory and comforting answer. This answer is found in 1 Thessalonians 4:13-18:

> But I would not have you to be ignorant, brethren, concerning them which are asleep, that ye sorrow not, even as others which have no hope. For if we believe that Jesus died and rose again, even so them also which sleep in Jesus will God bring with him. For this we say unto you by the word of the Lord, that we which are alive and remain unto the coming of the Lord shall not prevent them which are asleep. For the Lord himself shall descend from heaven with a shout, with the voice of the archangel, and with the trump of God; and the dead in Christ shall rise first: Then we which are alive and remain shall be caught up together with them in the clouds, to meet the Lord in the air; and so shall we ever be with the Lord. Wherefore comfort one another with these words.

The subject of this paragraph is "The Christian dead and their relation to the second coming of Christ." The information given in this paragraph is necessarily limited. It is by no means an exhaustive treatment on immortality, eschatology, or the life beyond. Some Bible students have been guilty of reading into this text far more than what is actually there. Some have even gone so far as to make this passage refer to a preliminary coming of Christ to rapture the saints out of the world before the period of great tribulation. Then, according to this theory, He will come again after the tribulation period (a third coming!). But there is nothing in this paragraph to indicate that Paul was referring to anything other than the one and only return of Christ to earth. He is simply showing one particular aspect of that coming, namely, that which is related to the Christian dead.

On the subject of "our Christian dead" Paul seems to present three topics for consideration: their present state; their part in the second coming of Christ; and our attitude in the light of these facts. The first is a bare abstruse hint. The other two are positively presented.

Their Present State

In approaching the subject of the relation of the Christian dead to the return of Christ, Paul uses a term which does give some hint as to their present state, a term which has also been misunderstood and misinterpreted by some. It is the word, "asleep." Paul refers to their Christian dead as "them which are asleep." Some have taken this to mean that the Christian dead are now in a state of "soul sleeping," a state of unconscious existence awaiting the return of Christ and the resurrection of the body. Such an interpretation does not coincide with other references in Paul's letters to the definite, conscious existence of the soul after death in a real and living experience. It is a dangerous thing to take one word which is incidental to the main subject and highly symbolic and build a system of theology around it. Those who have advocated the "soul-sleeping" idea have been guilty of this mistake.

Paul's use of the expression, "them which are asleep," is obviously symbolic. A little later in the same passage he refers to these as the "dead in Christ." Death as a sleeping was often expressed by both Jews and Christians. It has no reference to the unconscious existence of the soul. It does have reference to the resting of the body while awaiting the resurrection. If we limit ourselves to this one passage we dare not go beyond this in thinking of the present state of the Christian dead.

Their Part in the Second Coming of Christ

The present state of the Christian dead was not the main concern of the apostle in this particular paragraph of his epistle to the Thessalonians. The one paramount concern was the relation of these dead to the glorious return of the Lord to earth. Would they miss out on the glory and thrill of this blessed event? Neither was there grave concern or question concerning the fact of the resurrection of the body or the fact of the Lord's return. William Arnold Stevens, in *The American Commentary*, quotes the following interesting and accurate explanation from Lillie's Commentary:

> The idea that perplexed and distressed the Thessalonians seems to have been something of this sort: that when the Lord came, their deceased friends would be found to have suffered serious loss, in that, while they would ultimately, no doubt, be raised again, they would yet have no part in the joy of welcoming Him back to His inheritance of the redeemed earth, and in the triumphant inauguration of his reign.[1]

To enlighten their troubled minds Paul called the attention of these Thessalonian Christians to three glorious facts. First, these beloved dead, instead of being left out, will be the first on the scene when the Lord comes again, for the Lord will bring these with Him at His coming. They will be in a much better position to enjoy and exult in this glorious appearing than their Christian friends who have been left behind on earth. According to the *King James Version*, Paul says, "For this we say unto you by the word of the Lord, that we which are alive and remain unto the coming of the Lord shall not prevent them which are asleep." The verb, "prevent," does not do justice to the original language. Dr. Ray Summers explains that "it was Paul's way of saying that when the Lord returns the living Christians will have no advantage whatever, no privilege whatever, beyond that of the Christians who will have fallen asleep before His return."[2] The word which Paul uses here, literally translated, means "to come before, precede, or anticipate." In other words, the dead in Christ will have favored position when the Lord returns.

Second, these beloved dead would join in the celebration of the victory of the returning Lord. The details of this victory celebration of our Lord are not clearly outlined in this passage, but the implication is that these deceased Christians would not only be present to witness it but also have a part in it. When these redeemed of the Lord come with Him at His return there will be a shout, the voice of the archangel, and the sound of the trumpet of God. We may well imagine that these beloved dead will have a part in that shout which will announce the coming of our Lord.

Third, these beloved dead will be reunited with their living loved ones when they meet the Lord in the air. Those who are still living "shall be caught up together with them in the clouds." And together we shall be with the Lord forever. This must have been a welcome and blessed thought to those distressed Christians of Thessalonica. The thought of seeing their deceased loved ones again was, indeed, a blessed thought, but the idea of meeting them at the coming of the Lord for a joint celebration of the Lord's glorious triumph was doubly blessed. They were not only thrilled at the fact of seeing their loved ones again, but they were also thrilled as to the occasion of this happy reunion.

Our Attitude in the Light of These Facts

Since Paul was talking to Christians who were living on this earth at the time, we may appropriately apply the lesson to those of us who are now living on this earth. What attitude should we have toward those who have gone on? What about our attitude toward those who have preceded us in death, especially our own dear friends and loved ones? We speak, of course, concerning those who have died in Christ. What Paul said to these Christians does not apply to loved ones who may have died outside of Christ. We speak only of the Christian dead. With reference to our attitude toward these Christian dead and the return of Christ, the apostle offers four suggestions.

First, we are not to sorrow as those who have no hope. "That ye sorrow not, even as others which have no hope." Dr. Summers, in his interpretation of this passage, explains that "Paul did not tell the Thessalonians that they were not to grieve for lost loved ones. Grief is normal for one who has lost a loved one in death; in many cases it has proved to have genuine value. Paul did say, however, that when Christian loved ones were lost in death, sorrow for them was not to be hopeless because an element of hope has been introduced into human experience."[3]

There is a difference between hopeless sorrowing and hopeful sorrowing. Even where Christians are concerned there will be sorrow because of the absence of a dear loved one, but that sorrow will be appreciably attenuated by the hope of a happy reunion at the coming of the glorified Son of God. For a true Christian this sorrow will have its sting, but the hope of a blessed reunion on the happy occasion of the return of our Lord will overshadow and soon completely obliterate the sorrow. At least, this is the way it should be if we follow the advice of the apostle as given in this text.

Second, we should look forward with happy anticipation to this reunion in glory. It is more than just a matter of attenuating our sorrow; rather, it is a matter of completely changing our sorrow into happy anticipation. The sorrow is overcome, not so much by a mere squelching of the sorrow, but by a replacing of the sorrow with happy anticipation. Instead of being sorrowful without hope Paul urges his Thessalonian friends to look with joy and happy expectation to that day which will soon come when their deceased loved ones will come in glory with the Lord, and all the redeemed shall meet Him in the air.

Third, we are to share this comfort with one another. It is possible to have a source of comfort which is not realized. The comfort of which we speak is that which comes through knowledge. It is not instinctively lodged in the human mind. The human mind has an instinctive tendency to be sorrowful when loved ones pass away. The only way we can overcome this sorrow is to gain information which the world does not have. It is information which has come through divine inspiration.

Paul assured these Christians that the information which he brought was "the word of the Lord." We have no record of any such word coming from the lips of Jesus as recorded in the Gospels. Paul must have meant that he had received this information by special divine revelation. We cannot doubt that he did. This information that Paul received by special divine revelation, he passed on to his Christian friends that, in the consciousness of this knowledge, they might have a source of comfort which heretofore they did not have.

And then Paul urged these same readers to pass this information on to others, even as he had done to them. There were others who needed this information, without which they would find themselves overcome with sorrow when death took their loved ones. It is only in the consciousness of this information and by implicit faith in its reliability that we can find the comfort we need when we think of our deceased friends. Christians need not wallow in the gloom of sorrow. There is light; there is hope. Let us rejoice in this hope and share this good news with others.

Fourth, since the subject of the return of Christ had been introduced as it relates to the Christian dead, Paul felt it expedient that he take advantage of the occasion to give another exhortation concerning our preparation for that coming. This is what the apostle did in the first part of the following chapter, the fifth.

In discussing with the Thessalonian Christians the relationship of their beloved dead to the second coming of Christ, Paul anticipated a question which he knew they were bound to ask. This anticipated question concerned the time of the return of our Lord to earth. This is the question that Christians through the ages have been asking. It is the question the disciples asked Jesus on the Mount of Olives. It is the question which they asked the resurrected Christ just before His ascension. The subject of the second coming of Christ is never presented except that some one will raise the question, "When?" The apostle Paul was perfectly safe in assuming that the people would raise such a question.

In answering this question Paul simply reminded his readers that they already knew all they needed to know concerning the time of our Lord's return. "But of the times and the seasons, brethren, ye have no need that I write unto you. For yourselves know perfectly that the day of the Lord so cometh as a thief in the night" (5:1,2). It is also all that is necessary for us to know. Natural human curiosity is always seeking for more information concerning the details of His coming, but all that we really need to know we already know. There is much that we need to know with reference to Christian life and Christian service, and we should be constantly on the alert to gain more knowledge in these areas, but in the matter of the time of our Lord's coming we must learn to be satisfied with the knowledge we already have—that the Lord will come as a thief in the night.

This is the same message which Jesus gave His disciples in that Olivet address. It was there that the analogy of the thief was first introduced. It merely means that He will come at a time when we least expect it. In view of that fact Paul offers three suggestions concerning our preparation for the return of Christ. These are basically the same as those given by Jesus to His disciples in Olivet. Let us look at them briefly in passing.

First, in the light of the unexpected nature of the coming of Christ, Paul's admonition was this: "Therefore let us not sleep as do others; but let us watch and be sober" (5:6). From the spiritual standpoint we live in the daytime. There is no night for those who have been born into the life of light. "But ye, brethren, are not in darkness, that that day should overtake you as a thief. Ye are all the children of light, and the children of the day: we are not of the night, nor of darkness" (5:4,5). In Christ we live in an eternal day. The day was made for opened eyes, and we who live in this spiritual day should never close the eyes of our hearts, that is, we should keep our minds and hearts alert to spiritual dangers, opportunities, and expectations. But we must do more than merely keep our eyes open; we must look earnestly for His appearing. The Christian should be ever mindful of the possible appearing of our Lord in glory, and our hearts should constantly breathe the atmosphere of joyful expectancy with reference to that coming.

Second, along with watching we must be sober. Our preparation for the second coming of Christ involves a sober watching. The word that Paul used here carries the idea of being calm and collected in spirit. It means that we should live so as to have access to the fullest measure of our own faculties. Any kind of conduct or action which interferes with or limits the full use of our faculties of mind, body, and soul is not in keeping with sobriety. If we are to prepare adequately for His coming, we must always have at our command the full use of our faculties.

Third, the third phase of our preparation for the coming of the Lord, according to Paul in this passage, is an active participation in serving one another. Paul closed this admonition concerning the return of the Lord by saying, "Wherefore comfort yourselves together, and edify one another, even as also ye do" (5:11). This service to one another is to be in the form of comfort and edification. The comfort is to be achieved by reminding one another of the promise of the return of our Lord. To edify is to "build up" or "strengthen." This work of edification may take any one of many different forms, but, generally speaking, it includes anything that one may do to strengthen the faith and character of another Christian.

In recapitulation let us restate Paul's recipe for preparation in the light of the imminent return of our Lord: watch, be sober, and serve one another. By following these three simple words of exhortation we will find life fuller and richer, and then at the appearing of our Lord our position will be more delightful and glorious. The big question is not *when* He will appear, but will I be ready when He does appear?

8
THE MAN OF SIN

The apostle Paul spoke to the Thessalonian Christians in his First Epistle about being ready and watching for the return of the Lord Jesus. They interpreted this to mean that He would definitely come within the week or the month. Many of them ceased their labor and sat gazing into the sky. Not only had they created an economic problem by their cessation of work, but they were also creating a spiritual and theological problem by their constant wrangling over the details of the Lord's coming. The Second Letter was written by Paul to correct this false interpretation.

In this Second Letter Paul explained to his Christian friends that he did not mean to leave the impression that Jesus would definitely come on that day or that week. Certain things would first have to transpire: a great apostasy; the revealing of the man of sin; and the taking away of the one who restrains. Here for the first time Paul steps into the role of a prophet and delves into the future of life on this earth. As in most prophetic utterances the details are not spelled out. What Paul said is bound to be true, but just exactly what he meant is not clear. The general outline is discernible, but we must beware of pressing the details too far.

Usually in interpreting the message of Paul we can speak with certainty and sure-footedness, but in this case we must confess that we are on ground that is not especially firm. Fortunately, however, it is not necessary for us to have all of the details in our possession. It is well enough for us to know the bare outline and the fundamental principles that underlie these prophetic utterances. Of these we can be sure. We shall go as far as we can in understanding the details of the picture, even to the point of offering some proposed interpretations with certain reservations.

The most prominent feature of 2 Thessalonians is the reference to "the man of sin." Who is this man of sin? What will he do? When will he come? What will be his destiny? These are questions which men through the ages have tried to answer on the basis of what Paul has written in this chapter. Some attempts have been made to associate Paul's words with other apocalyptic and prophetic utterances found in the New Testament, such as in Matthew 24 and 25 and in the Revelation. There could be some relationship, but we should be extremely cautious in identifying these apocalyptic passages. This is about the only passage to be found in Paul's writings which could be called prophetic so far as life on this earth is concerned, except for a few incidental references here and there. Looking at this passage in 2 Thessalonians we shall attempt to determine four facts about this man of sin: his character; his work; his time; and his identity.

His Character

What kind of a person is this man of sin as described by Paul? Gathering up the information which is given to us throughout the passage we arrive at five summary conclusions. *First, he has no respect for law.* Literally, the phrase should read "the man of lawlessness." He has no regard or respect for law. This, of course, is the essence of sin. *Second, he is opposed to God.* Being lawless he would naturally be opposed to God since God is the very essence of law. Paul describes him as the one "who opposeth." *Third, he deifies himself.* Not only does he oppose God, but he also claims to be God. He takes the place of God and claims for himself all of the attributes of deity. "And exalteth himself above all that is called God, or that is worshipped; so that he as God sitteth in the temple of God, showing himself that he is God" (2:4).

Fourth, he is able to work wonders. He appears to have power to do unusual things. His coming, said Paul, "is after the working of Satan with all power and signs and lying wonders" (2:9). His is no ordinary power. He is possessed of super-human strength. *And finally, he is deceptive.* His nature is that of deception. His whole life is based upon subterfuge. He accomplishes his desired ends through deception. Paul explained to the Thessalonians that his coming is with "all deceivableness or unrighteousness in them that perish" (2:10).

His Work

This man of sin is engaged in the work of turning men from God to himself as the one object of worship. By every means in keeping with his satanic character he goes about to turn men from God. The turning away, it appears, is the result of his work. Some interpret the turning away and the revealing of the man of sin as two separate and distinct events. Dr. W. A. Stevens,[1] for example, thinks that the "falling away" refers to a development within the church and the appearing of "the man of sin" as a development outside the church. But I am of the impression that the two events are related as cause and effect. "Let no man deceive you by any means; for that day shall not come, except there come a falling away first, and that man of sin be revealed, the son of perdition" (2:3). Paul speaks of the falling away first, and then he mentions the revealing of the man of sin as an explanation of the falling away. We would not be dogmatic at this point, but the total picture indicates that the business of this man of sin is to turn the people away from God and to establish himself in the mind of man as the only true object of worship. If this is his business, he has been exceedingly successful in it.

His Time

When does this man of sin make his appearance? What of the time of his coming? Many Bible students have interpreted this passage to mean that there will come this man of sin at some future day in the history of the world, just preceding the second advent of our Lord, but Paul makes it plain in our text that this man of sin is already at work in the world. He is not speaking of one who will come at some later date; he speaks of one who is already here. "For the mystery of iniquity doth already work" (2:7). The word for "iniquity" here is the same word as found in the phrase, "man of sin."

Paul does speak of something that is future, but it is the revealing of the man of sin, not his coming. He is already at work in the world, but at some future time his identity will be made known. This is the event that will take place just prior to the return of Jesus.

At the moment (at least it was true in Paul's day) there is a restraining power that keeps him from exercising all of the power he would like to have. Paul spoke of the one "who now letteth" (2:7). He also suggested that the Christians of Thessalonica knew who restrained the power of the man of sin (verse 6). While the man of sin is at work in our world, there is a power that holds him back. Just what this restraining power is we will try to figure out a little later, but suffice it to say at this point that there will come a time, according to Paul, when this restraining power will be lifted. Then the man of sin will be revealed in all the fullness of his power, bringing in the great apostasy.

His Identity

Now we are ready to tackle the real problem: Who is this man of sin? This is not to suggest that we will come up with an undeniable answer. There have been many speculations with reference to this answer. There are almost as many different answers as there are theologians. We do not claim to have anything new on the subject nor have we been able to come up with any new clues. We can only give what appears to be the most reasonable answer. In order to make ourselves clear it will help to give a brief summary of the predominant views that have been given in the commentaries on this subject.

First, there are those, like W. A. Stevens[2] and F. Godet,[3] who hold that the man of sin refers to Pharisaic Judaism. In this case the one who restrains would be the Roman government, which held the Jews in check. Such a view is certainly possible in the light of the text, and yet it does not seem to be the most plausible explanation.

Second, there are those who, like B. H. Carroll,[4] hold that the man of sin is the Roman Catholic Church as expressed in the papacy. In this case the one who restrains would be the existing moral or legal order. This position fits into the post-millennial interpretation of eschatology. However, if the man of sin was already at work in Paul's day, it would be difficult to fit in the idea of the papacy since there was no papacy as such until almost the seventh century (590 A.D.).

A third position is held by most of those who are identified with premillennial eschatology. This position identifies the man of sin with a coming personal antichrist who would make himself a rival to Christ for man's worship and devotion. According to this view a distinction is made between the "principle" which was already at work in Paul's day and the "person" who will come at the end time. In this case the one who restrains is the government which will keep the antichrist in check and oppose his coming for full power. When that restraint is removed, however, the antichrist will be seen in his true nature and will be destroyed by Christ at His coming.

While all of these positions have some merit the one which seems to be the most reasonable and appropriate to me is that suggested as a possibility by Dr. Ray Summers in his book, *The Life Beyond*. Dr. Summers has also given a splendid summary of the leading views. His suggestion is that "the man of sin is Satan himself. He was working in Paul's day and was destined to grow in power until 'in his own season' his true character would be unveiled, and he would be destroyed by Christ at His coming."[5] The one who restrains is the Holy Spirit. He keeps Satan from exercising his full power. One day he will release that restraint, and Satan will be seen in his true character. Then Christ will come and destroy him. This explanation is not free from problems, but it does seem to give the best overall picture. We human beings are prone to relate all such predictions to human personalities.

There will be human personalities involved, and certain human personalities will be especially used by Satan in his work from generation to generation. It would be proper to classify any man as "the man of sin" who personifies the spirit and nature of Satan.

There is little to be gained by a lengthy argument that seeks to prove the identity of the man of sin with any one person or event. There is much to be gained, however, by a serious consideration of the abiding principles or lessons clearly discernible in this apocalyptic message. Let us give emphasis to three fundamental lessons that may be derived from this passage of scripture concerning the future.

First, the forces of wickedness are at work in our world. We need not wait until some future day to see the moving of the forces of evil against the people of God. We must all recognize that we are in a terrific struggle with the forces of evil. This is not a battle which will be fought by our descendants in some future age. It is an ever-present struggle requiring the best defense we can put up.

Second, those who are not truly anchored to Christ will be deceived, and many will fall away. Whether or not we are in the period of the great apostasy is not the major issue. Whether it is going on now or is yet to come, the fact to remember is that only those who are superficially tied onto Christ will be caught away in this apostasy. There is good reason to believe that in this day of a popular Christianity many people are becoming identified with the Christian movement who have no vital relationship to Christ. In the day of the great apostasy these will be easy prey for the man of sin. They will fall away from a faith which they appeared to have. But this one verity is sure—those who are anchored to Christ in genuine faith cannot be turned away from Him. Paul makes this clear in the thirteenth verse: "But we are bound to give thanks always to God for you, brethren beloved of the Lord, because God hath from the beginning chosen you to salvation through sanctification of the Spirit and belief of the truth." There will be no exodus of the genuinely redeemed, but there will be a vast exodus of those who had only a superficial relationship to Christ and Christianity.

Third, this force of evil, whether in principle or in person, will be finally destroyed forever at the coming of Christ. The man of sin may exert his superhuman power and lead many astray by his deception, but he is doomed, sooner or later, to destruction. It behooves every person to anchor himself by faith to the eternal Rock of Ages who will withstand all the assaults of Satan and finally turn all the elements of destruction upon him. There are perilous days ahead. Many will fall, but blessed are those who have anchored themselves to this mighty Rock of Ages.

9
THE RESURRECTION OF THE BODY

Any study of Paul's eschatology would be incomplete without a consideration of his matchless discourse on the resurrection of the body in Corinthians 15. It is a masterpiece of oratory, as well as a fantastic revelation of an event yet to occur at the end of the age. In this particular discourse Paul does not specify the exact time in the schedule of age-end events that this resurrection of the body will occur, but the implication all the way through is that it will take place in connection with the return of our Lord.

First Corinthians 15 constitutes the fourth main division of the Epistle. Throughout the Epistle Paul deals with the problems faced by the Corinthian Church. One of these was fellowship; another was moral conduct; a third dealt with public worship; and the fourth concerned the resurrection of the body. The rising tide of Gnosticism had created doubts in the minds of some Christians as to the reality and nature of the resurrected body. There had probably been many heated discussions on this subject. The message the apostle delivered in this chapter was designed to resolve these doubts. It is the greatest essay ever written on the subject of the resurrection.

The apostle begins by reaffirming the fact of the resurrection of Christ. All hope of the bodily resurrection of the believer is based on the fact of the bodily resurrection of Jesus. The only proper place, therefore, to begin a discussion on the resurrection of the believer is at the point of the historical fact of the resurrection of Jesus. Even the Gnostic skeptics who doubted the bodily resurrection of the believer accepted the fact of the resurrection of

Jesus. To begin with, the historical fact was appropriate from two points of view: It was a common ground on which all could agree, and it was the true basis for all hope in the believer's bodily resurrection.

In verses 12 through 34 Paul points out the advantages of a hope in the resurrection of the body. Hope is the expectation of some good thing which one does not possess or experience at the moment. Hope always has reference to the future. In the Christian religion, hope is a prominent feature. Hope is an indispensable element in life, and anything that contains or offers hope is attractive to the human heart. On this basis alone the Christian religion holds an attraction for most of those who know of it.

There are many areas of hope in the Christian faith, but the one Paul has in mind in our text is that which concerns the resurrection of the body at the consummation of the age and the return of Christ. We are not thinking of the continuous and unbroken life of the soul which transcends death. The flight of the soul from earth to heaven is not a resurrection. The soul never ceases to live; therefore, it cannot be resurrected. At death the soul of the Christian simply is transported to a new location and environment. There is no break in its existence.

But at death the body dies and is buried. It returns to the dust whence it came. Death means cessation of being. The soul, once born into the kingdom of God, never experiences death. The life of the soul is eternal life without interruption, but not so with the physical body. It does die and it ceases to exist as a living organism.

The hope of which Paul speaks is the hope of the resurrection of this body. All through the chapter the subject of discussion is the body, not the soul. We must keep in mind the distinction. It is not immortality alone of which we speak. One may believe in the immortality of the soul without believing in the resurrection of the body. Christian hope is more than belief in immortality; it is belief in the resurrection of the body. We can live without a body, but it is doubtlessly better to live in a body. Therefore, there is much consolation for the Christian to know that his body will be resurrected and reunited with the soul. This hope, Paul tells us in verses 20 through 34, assures us of victory over death; it assures us of a reunion with Christian loved ones who are dead; and it gives incentive and courage for fidelity in Christian responsibility in spite of opposition and hindrances.

Having established the fact of the resurrection of the body and the practical significance of this hope, the apostle proceeds, in verses 35 to 50, to answer another question which had been raised by some of the Corinthians. The question was this: If there is to be a resurrection of the body, what will be the nature of it? What kind of a body will it be? "But some man will say, How are the dead raised up? And with what body do they come?" (verse 35). In answering these questions Paul demonstrates his remarkable ability as a logician. Even though he is dealing with the metaphysical and that which is yet to come, he draws upon the persuasive powers of sound reason in describing the nature of the resurrection body. It is the clearest picture in the New Testament of the resurrection of the body.

In concise categorical form the apostle directs the minds of his readers in five successive steps or conclusions concerning the resurrection body. He readily admits that there are details which our finite minds are incapable of grasping, but there are other aspects which we can understand, at least in general outline. The five progressive steps or statements are as follow:

The Body Cannot Be Resurrected Until It Dies

Paul begins by rebuking the Corinthian skeptics with these words: "Thou fool, that which thou sowest is not quickened, except it die" (verse 36). Evidently these critics were denying the possibility of the resurrection of the body simply on the basis that they had never seen a resurrected body. Of course, they had not seen one because it must be preceded by death. Paul draws his analogy from the grain of corn or wheat. It must first be put into the ground, and then it dies. Out of that death comes resurrection in the form of the stalk. Jesus Himself had used this same analogy in teaching the Greeks who came to see Him in Jerusalem. To these seekers He spoke of the necessity of His death and said, "Except a corn of wheat fall into the ground and die, it abideth alone; but if it die, it bringeth forth much fruit" (John 12:24). As in the resurrection of the grain, so also in the resurrection of the human body, there must be death before there can be resurrection. Death is the region through which the body must go before it can rise again.

It Will Be Different from the Present Body

It is difficult for us to understand the details of this difference, but from the analogy of the grain of corn we can see at least the general idea. Just as the stalk of corn which shoots forth out of the ground is different from the grain of corn which was put in the ground, so shall our resurrected bodies be different from our present bodies. Paul's explanation is as follows: "so also is the resurrection of the dead. It is sown in corruption; it is raised in incorruption: it is sown in dishonour; it is raised in glory; it is sown in weakness; it is raised in power" (vv. 42, 43).

Paul does not try to explain the difference, except to affirm that it will be different. This is not to claim that there will not be some mark of identity in order that we may be recognized in our resurrected state, but there will be a marked difference. This may account for the fact that some of Jesus' closest associates failed to recognize Him when He appeared in His resurrected form. Mary did not recognize Him; neither did the two men on the road to Emmaus. Apparently He had been changed. In what manner we cannot declare, but the fact of a change is verified by their failure to identify Him at first glance. In time they were able to identify Him. Even so, we also shall be changed in the resurrection, but not to the extent that we will lose all identity. The stalk of corn is different from the grain, but if you look closely enough on the stalk you will find ears which contain grains of corn; thereby you are able to identify it as corn. There will also be some such identification mark on the resurrected body.

It Will Not Be an Exact Duplicate of Another Body

Each redeemed person will retain his distinctive personality in the resurrection. We will not be carbon copies of one another. There will be as much variety among persons as now. There will be no monotonous similarities. Each will carry his own distinctive characteristics. It would certainly be less fascinating if we thought that all redeemed and resurrected bodies would be exactly alike. The apostle is careful to explain that this will not be the case: "But God giveth it a body as it hath pleased him, and to every seed his own body. All flesh is not the same flesh; but there is one kind of flesh of men, another flesh of beasts, another of fishes, and other of birds. There are also celestial bodies, and bodies terrestrial: but the glory of the celestial is one, and the glory of the terrestrial is another. There is one glory of the sun, and another glory of the moon, and another glory of the stars: for one star differeth from another star in glory" (verses 38-41).

All will be glorious in the resurrection, but there will be a variety of glory. The sun is different from the moon and yet both are majestic. Even the stars differ one from the other. So shall it be with the resurrection of the body. Each body will have its distinctive type of glory. The glory will thus be made all the more glorious by this endless variety.

It Will Be a Spiritual Body

Paul distinguishes between our natural bodies which we have now and our spiritual bodies which we shall possess in the resurrection. "It is sown a natural body; it is raised a spiritual body. There is a natural body, and there is a spiritual body. And so it is written, the first man Adam was made a living soul; the last Adam was made a quickening spirit. Howbeit that was not first which is spiritual, but that which is natural; and afterward that which is spiritual" (vv. 44-46).

The distinction which Paul makes here is not between the material and the spiritual, but between the physical or psychic and the spiritual. The word the apostle uses here is the word, *psyche*. It is the word from which we derive our word, "psychology." The *King James* translates it "natural," which may be about the best word for it. Edwards describes this natural body as "an organism fitted to be the seat of mind, to express emotion, to carry out the behests of will."[1] It is not the spiritual, but it has in it the making of the spiritual. It is capable of producing the spiritual. The difference between the natural and the spiritual is not that of the difference between bad and good but between the rudimentary and the finished product.

The material body is only the abode of the natural man. Paul's argument is that, since God has provided a body for the natural man, He will surely also provide a body for the spiritual man. The body for the natural man is suited to the physical being of man; even so the body for the spiritual man will be suited to the spiritual being. There is a sense in which man is a spiritual being, but the better word for its is *psyche* or "soul," which through redemption and death becomes truly spiritual. Therefore, the body which we inherit in the resurrection will be a spiritual body; at least it will be commensurate with the spiritual nature of the redeemed soul in glory.

In speaking of the first Adam as a living soul, Paul was thinking of this natural man, the physical man. The second Adam became a life-giving spirit. He must have been referring to Christ in His resurrected form. Before His resurrection Jesus was psychic, like Adam, but after His resurrection He became, not only a spirit, but a "life-giving" spirit. The first Adam, being physical, was given a body which was of this earth on which he lived. The second Adam, in His spiritual state, was given a body which was spiritual in nature, corresponding to the spiritual state in which He lives. "The first man is of the earth, earthy: the second man is the Lord from heaven. As is the earthy such are they also that are earthy; and as is the heavenly, such are they also that are heavenly" (vv.

47, 48). The word, earthy, denotes that which comes out of the ground. The earthly body is made of clay to correspond with the earthly type of existence, but the heavenly body will be spiritual to correspond with the nature of the heavenly type of existence. Paul's point of emphasis is that, if God provides a body for this earthly type of life, He will also provide a body for the heavenly type of life, but it will be a spiritual body to correspond with the type of life.

This does not mean that we will cease to be human beings in the resurrection. Our resurrected bodies will be spiritual and human, but not earthly, not flesh and blood. The corn does not cease to be corn when it springs forth from the ground in resurrection. Neither does the human being cease to be a human being when he springs forth after death in resurrection life. Flesh and blood are not indispensable qualities of human life. The human life we have on earth will blossom forth in new radiance on the resurrection day. It will be no less human then than now. Some people seem to have gotten the idea that in heaven we will cease to be humans and will become angels. This sentiment has been expressed in a song which was once popular. It went something like this: "I want to be an angel, and with the angel band . . ." I have no desire to be an angel. Why should anyone want to be an angel when, as redeemed children of God, we will hold a place in glory far above the angels. The angels will be our servants. No, we will not be angels in the resurrection; we will be glorified human beings in a spiritual state of existence.

It Will Be Glorious and Perfect in Every Respect

We cannot draw a picture of the resurrected body, nor can we draw a mental picture of it with our finite minds, but we can be assured that it will be glorious and perfect. This earthly body is full of imperfections and distractions, but the heavenly body will be free from all that mars. It is the difference between that which is corruptible and that which is incorruptible, between that which is dishonorable and that which is glorious, between that which is weak and that which is powerful. Paul reminds his readers that "as we have borne the image of the earthy, we shall also bear the image of the heavenly."

Some scholars have suggested that these words might best be translated as hortatory in form, making it read, "as we have borne the image of the earthy, let us also bear the image of the heavenly." From the standpoint of the verb form, this is a possible reading, but the context clearly precludes it. E. P. Gould is right in observing that the hortatory translation "makes a positive break in the discussion, nothing before leading up to it, and nothing following leading from it."[2]

This is simply the climactic statement in the conclusion of his argument showing the difference between the earthly body and the heavenly body which we shall receive in the resurrection. To bear the image of the heavenly is to possess the heavenly type of life. Just what changes will be made in our resurrected bodies we do not know, but we do know that whatever changes are made will be for the better. Our natural bodies are beset with weakness, infirmities, and imperfections; our heavenly bodies will be free from all such imperfections and weaknesses. We will all be beautiful. There will be no ugly bodies, no disfigured faces, no broken or disarranged limbs. With this reference to the heavenly body Paul waxes forth in a glorious tribute of praise and rejoicing for the hope which involves this resurrection experience. The very thought of it sends a tingle down the spine. It makes any sacrifice of this earthly existence seem trivial. How could any person be indifferent to the invitation which makes possible this blessed hope of a new and glorious body in the resurrection?

The closing verses of the 15th chapter of this Corinthian Epistle do not set forth any new ideas on the subject of the resurrection of the body; they merely express in climactic fashion the reaction of Paul's heart to the thought of it. It is a doxology coming from the overflow of the apostle's heart. It constitutes a fitting climax to this matchless discourse on the resurrection of the body.

The whole chapter is one of those mountaintop experiences in the writings of Paul, and this last paragraph is the highest peak on that mountain. It is that final crescendo which brings thrills and tingling to the spine in the presentation of the resurrection oratorio. There is poetic beauty and force, as well as a theologically sound content. Who can read it without being impressed with its forceful logic and poetic beauty?

> Now this I say, brethren, that flesh and blood cannot inherit the kingdom of God; neither doth corruption inherit incorruption. Behold, I show you a mystery; we shall not all sleep, but we shall all be changed. In a moment, in the twinkling of an eye, at the last trump: for the trumpet shall sound, and the dead shall be raised incorruptible, and we shall be changed. For this corruptible must put on incorruption, and this mortal must put on immortality. So when this corruptible shall have put on incorruption, and this mortal shall have put on immortality, then shall be brought to pass the saying that is written, Death is swallowed up in victory. O death, where is thy sting? O grave, where is thy victory? The sting of death is sin; and the strength of sin is the law. But thanks be to God, which giveth us the victory through our Lord Jesus Christ. Therefore, my beloved brethren, be ye steadfast, unmovable, always abounding in the work of the Lord, forasmuch as ye know that your labor is not in vain in the Lord (vv. 50-58).

Paul transplants himself in vision to that day when the dead shall be raised incorruptible—and tries to depict for us something of its glory. Even with his gifted pen it was difficult to do justice to the glory and majesty of it.

The passage begins with a reminder that we shall be changed in the resurrection, even those who are still living on this earth. Not all will have fallen asleep in death, for some will be living on the earth when our Savior appears to usher in the resurrection day. Those who are then living on the earth will not go through the experience of death, but they will go through an experience of metamorphosis. "we shall not all sleep, but we shall all be changed." This change will take place "in a moment, in the twinkling of an eye," but it must take place. No one will be allowed to enter into the joys of heaven in this earthly form of body. We must be changed, even those who have not died. Paul explains that "flesh and blood cannot inherit the kingdom of God" (v. 50).

This blessed day of resurrection, when this corruptible shall put on incorruption and this mortal shall put on immortality, will mark the final victory for the Christian. It will be a victory over death as prophesied a long time ago by the prophet Isaiah: "He will swallow up death in victory; and the Lord God will wipe away tears from off all faces; and the rebuke of his people shall he take away from off all the earth" (Isaiah 25:8). The apostle remembers this promise and refers in this chapter to its fulfillment on the resurrection day.

Part III
The Eschatology of Peter

10
THE END IS AT HAND

Even though there are some distinctive features in the eschatology of Jesus, Paul, Peter, and John, there is much that is common to all four, and at no point do they contradict one another. However, we do need to look at each one individually in order to catch the total New Testament picture. Therefore, at the risk of being somewhat repetitious, we turn to the Epistles of Peter for another look at the eschatological scene. In the last chapter of our study we shall attempt to put all four of these eschatological pictures together in one composite picture.

There are two passages which call for examination in our study of the eschatology of Peter. The first is a brief passage in the fourth chapter of his First Epistle, and the second is a more lengthy passage covering the whole third chapter of his Second Epistle.

In his First Epistle, Peter repeatedly urges his readers to be faithful in religious exercises and moral responsibilities. He strengthens these exhortations by pointing first to the example of Jesus and then to the imminence of His return and the end of the age. In the fourth chapter we find an assertion of a fact and then an exhortation based upon and growing out of that fact. It reads as follows:

> But ye therefore sober, and watch unto prayer. And above all things have fervent charity among yourselves: for charity shall cover the multitude of sins. Use hospitality one to another without grudging. As every man hath received the gift, even so minister the same one to another, as good stewards of the manifold grace of

God. If any man speak, let him speak as the oracles of God; if any man minister, let him do it as of the ability which God giveth: that God in all things may be glorified through Jesus Christ: to whom be praise and dominion for ever and ever. Amen. (4:7-9).

This exhortation was introduced by a simple assertion: "The end of all things is at hand." The assertion was not intended to be the most prominent feature of the paragraph. It was introduced only as a basis for the exhortation which followed; however, it is an astounding assertion and has attracted much attention by all students of the Epistle.

What did Peter mean by this statement? There is no problem, of course, at the point of understanding the terminology or syntax. It is a simple sentence using simple language, and yet there are some things about it which are somewhat perplexing. By "things" was he referring to this physical universe? This seems to be the obvious meaning, and, if so, he must have been thinking of the dissolution of this world order. The Greek word for "at hand" is a word which carries the idea of that which is near. Williams' translation seems to bring out these ideas most clearly: "But the end of everything on earth is near."[1]

The most serious problem here is not in relation to the understanding of the terminology but in the accuracy of the statement. Was the end of all things really at hand? Peter uttered these words nearly two thousand years ago, and the world still stands. It would appear that Peter was mistaken. If so, he was not alone. There are frequent references in the New Testament to the idea of the imminence of the end of the world. In a subsequent chapter we will have occasion to consider the simple statement of John, "It is the last hour." In most instances these references are associated with the second advent of Christ to earth. Though nothing is said in this particular passage about the return of Christ to earth, Peter makes it quite clear in his Second Epistle that he considered the end of all things as that which will take place in connection with the second coming of Christ to earth (2 Peter 3:10).

Most of the writers of the New Testament expressed at one time or another their belief in the imminence of this return of our Lord and with it the end of all things on earth. If Peter, then, was mistaken, so were the other apostles and preachers of the first century. But were they really mistaken? No. From the standpoint of actual time as we count time we could say that they were wrong in predicting the imminence of the end, but from the standpoint of possibility they were not at all wrong.

The coming of the Lord is always near in the sense that it is always possible. An elderly mother could say in all truthfulness that the coming of her son for a visit with her was imminent, even though he might not actually come in the door for days or weeks. His coming was imminent because she knew that he was passing nearby every day and could at any moment come in. In some such sense, the second coming of Christ is imminent. His coming is always possible. It is never wrong, therefore, to state that the end of all things is near. It is near because it could transpire at any moment. And as Christians we should always think of it as being near. The possibility that He may not come for another 2,000 years would not in any wise take anything away from the truthfulness of the statement that the end of all things is near. Though He has not yet come in His glory to consummate the end of the age, He is near enough that He could come at any moment. This is in reality an imminent coming.

The thought of this imminence of the coming of the end of the age should do something to a Christian. It should cause him to take more seriously the responsibilities the Lord has laid on him. In the light of this nearness of the end Peter presses the claims of Christ upon his readers. The thought of the nearness of the end doubtlessly caused them to give more attention to the exhortations thus given by the apostle. What should we do in the light of the imminence of the end of time? Peter answers this question by suggesting five approaches to his readers.

First, we should be sober. To be sober is to be serious minded. It simply means that we should take life seriously. This is no time for frivolous living. This does not mean that Christians should never have any kind of wholesome fun or recreation. One may do this on occasion and still hold in his heart a serious attitude toward life, and all the more in the light of the nearness of the end of all things.

Second, the consciousness of the nearness of the end of time should drive us to our knees in prayer. We are to "watch unto prayer." The nearness of the end calls for a nearness to Him who is coming to consummate the end. Real sober thinking usually issues in a deeper prayer life.

Third, with the imminent approach of the end of time, love for one another should help us experience genuine revival. "Above all things have fervent charity among yourselves: for charity shall cover a multitude of sins." We usually do not learn the true value of love until we see the things of this world slipping from our grasp. Love is more valuable than gold, but usually we do not realize this until the gold is just about gone. When we come, as did Peter and the other apostles, to live in the consciousness of the imminent end of all these things of the world, love for one another will be given a more prominent place in our thinking and acting. Certainly Peter did not mean that our love for others would cover our sins in the eyes of God. The only thing he could have meant is that our love for others will often be the means of curtailing or cutting off sinful tendencies on the part of those whom we love. Love does cut down on sin, whereas hate breeds sin. True brotherly love can do much to curtail the sinful tendencies of mankind.

Fourth, in the light of the imminence of the end we should be good stewards of that which God has placed in our hands. The end of time means that we will be called into account for the way we have used what God has placed in our hands. "As every man hath received the gift, even so minister the same one to another, as good stewards of the manifold grace of God." The fact that this time is near should cause us to re-evaluate our stewardship responsibilities.

Fifth, the nearness of the end of time should revive within us a sense of faithfulness in declaring the oracles of God. "If any man speak, let him speak as the oracles of God." It is ours to deliver and interpret to our world the message of God. Peter reminds his readers of this responsibility and intensifies it by calling their attention to the nearness of the end of time. This is our task, and its urgency grows more acute as we become aware of the proximity of His return.

Just as it was in the days of Simon Peter, the appearing of our Lord and the end of all things are near. It behooves us, therefore, to be sober, prayerful, loving, and faithful in stewardship and in the proclamation of the Word of the Lord. There is nothing that can shake our complacency like the reawakening of our hearts to the solemn fact of the nearness of the end. It may be trite, but it is true—It is later than you think! Would it make any difference in your life, if you knew that today would be your last day on this earth? Do you realize that this possibility is awfully close to reality?

11
THE DELAY OF THE SECOND COMING

The theme running through the third chapter of 2 Peter is the second coming of Christ. Several aspects of it are brought into focus, such as its delay, its prospect, and its issues. In this chapter we are concerned with the first of these.

In the first part of the chapter the apostle Peter recognizes a problem which had been raised by certain skeptic mockers and proceeds to answer their charge. This problem concerned the apparent delay in the return of Christ in the face of the many promises which had been made through the prophets and apostles of His imminent return.

The Fact of Its Delay

Peter begins by recognizing the fact that the return of Christ had been delayed beyond the expectation of many who looked for it in the weeks or months following His ascension. This delay had given the critics and enemies of Christianity a tool with which to prod and embarrass the Christians. Many of these critics went up and down the land, saying, "Where is the promise of his coming? For since the fathers fell asleep, all things continue as they were from the beginning of the creation" (v. 4).

Peter does not deny the fact that the return of Christ had been delayed beyond the time of his own expectation, but he does take the opportunity to correct an error in the charge of the critics. In order to emphasize the failure of the promise to return, they had pointed out that since the fathers had died all things have remained as they were from the beginning of creation. Even though they were right in pointing to the delay in Christ's coming, they were not right in arguing that things had remained as they were from the beginning of creation.

"Since the fathers fell asleep" must be a reference to the death of some of the original disciples of Jesus; however, some think that it refers to the patriarchal fathers of the Old Testament. The former seems to make better sense in the light of the context, for both Paul and Peter had preached that Jesus would return to the earth immediately. Since these promises were first made, many of the leaders of the Christian movement had died. At the time of this writing it had been some thirty to forty years since Jesus ascended with the promise that He would come again soon. Yet there was no sign of His coming, and the skeptical critics were quick to "rub it in" on the Christians.

But these skeptics were wrong in saying that everything had remained just as it was from the beginning of creation. Peter reminds them that God had brought an ordered universe out of chaos, but this created world was radically changed by a deluge of rain. There was a new beginning after this flood. This was only one of many changes which have taken place on this earth since the beginning of creation, but it was sufficient to show the fallacy of the charge which had been made by these garrulous critics.

There must have been some satisfaction in being able to show this fallacy in the thinking of his critics, but the charge of delay in the coming of Christ, Peter could not deny. Still less can we deny it after nearly 2,000 years. If the critics of Christianity mocked the Christians because of the failure of Jesus to return after thirty or forty years, how much more reason do the critics of our generation have for mocking? Nearly 2,000 years ago the followers of Christ preached that Jesus would come again very soon. Twenty centuries have passed, and still He has not appeared. What can we say in answer to the mockery of our critics? We cannot deny the delay; we can only recognize it.

The Disappointment in Its Delay

To the first-century Christians this was a real disappointment, for they longed for the return of Christ to earth in glory and actually expected it in their lifetime. However, this is not necessarily true of the average present-day Christian. There are very few Christians of our day who really expect Him to come in this generation. Most Christians still believe that He is coming again, but they think of it as an event in the distant future. This may be a somewhat normal reaction from the fact that He did not come during the first century when the Christians really expected Him. Now we are not so much disappointed that He has not yet come as we are embarrassed as we try to explain why He did not come in the first century as the disciples seemed to believe that He would. The skeptic still enjoys harassing the Christian with challenges concerning the delay in the promised return of Christ to earth.

The Reason for Its Delay

Though, at first, we may be somewhat chagrined by this delay, we are not without an answer for our critics, just as Simon Peter was not without an answer. The apostle's answer was reasonable, forceful, and significant:

"But, beloved, be not ignorant of this one thing, that one day is with the Lord as a thousand years, and a thousand years as one day. The Lord is not slack concerning his promise, as some men count slackness; but is long-suffering to usward, not willing that any should perish, but that all should come to repentance" (vv. 8, 9).

According to this answer from the pen of the apostle Peter there are two factors to be considered when we think of the delay in the return of Christ. *First, there is the difference between our way of counting time and God's way of counting time.* Time is not the same to God as it is to us. What we consider to be a thousand years may be only a day as God counts time, or our day may be to

Him a thousand years. Perhaps this idea was suggested to the mind of the apostle by the psalmist who sang, "For a thousand years in thy sight are but as yesterday when it is past, and as a watch in the night" (Psalm 90:4). It would be good if all Bible students would keep this differential in mind in interpreting the words of the apostle John in the twentieth chapter of the Apocalypse concerning the millennium, instead of insisting that this must be a literal reign on earth of a literal one thousand years as man counts time.

If, indeed, a thousand years is as a day with God, then Jesus has delayed His coming only two days! After all, what are a thousand years in the light of eternity? It's only a moment. So actually, the delay is not as long as it may appear to us from our limited vantage point. After all, the promises of Christ's return to earth must have been given in the Bible according to God's reckoning of time, and not ours.

The second factor which Peter points out in his answer to the question of his critics, "Where is the promise of His coming?" is the longsuffering of God. Christ has delayed His coming in order that more people might be prepared for that coming. It is an act of mercy. Some would gripe that God is lack or slow in keeping His promise, but this is not the case at all. It is just that God is merciful and longsuffering, "not willing that any should perish, but that all should come to repentance."

Should Christ come at this moment, it would be disastrous for millions who have not recognized His lordship. Every moment that He delays is one more opportunity for the unbeliever to make the preparation which is necessary to be blessed by His coming. Instead of wondering why God has seemed to delay the return of His Son to earth, we should welcome the opportunity this delay affords for evangelism and faith.

The Lord is concerned about His creatures, and He has gladly gone the second and third miles in order to induce men to receive the benefits that have been offered to all in Christ. He has even delayed the return of His Son to earth in order that more people might have the opportunity to receive Him before it is too late.

By way of a momentary parenthetical digression let me hasten to explain that these words of Peter are not to be interpreted to teach the doctrine of universalism. Some have so interpreted them to mean that all will finally be saved. When Peter wrote that the Lord is "not willing that any should perish," he was not teaching that God has so purposed. The word, "willing," carries the idea of inclination, not purpose. The comment of N. M. Williams is apropos at this point:

> God's disposition is such that He has no desire in itself that men perish. . . . Peter here has nothing to say concerning that eternal and loving purpose by which the sufferings of the Son are prevented from being borne in vain; but he is accounting for the delay of Christ's coming to judge the world. The judgment is delayed, in order that, if possible, all men may be saved. If men are lost before Christ comes, it is not because no opportunity to be saved is given them.[1]

The delay of Christ in coming back to earth means two things: *First, it means that God has given to us another chance to make known the glorious gospel of redemption through His shed blood.* Every Christian should consider every day's delay as such. When our Lord comes again to earth, we will have no more opportunity to share the gospel message with those who are lost.

It is not that He wants to give us more time to live on this earth, for there is something far better to be experienced by those who believe when our Savior comes again. He delays His coming for this reason only—to give us another chance to share the story of redemption with someone who is now lost in sin. What are we doing with these precious days of grace which He has given to us for this purpose? It is sad to think that we have already passed up many opportunities to witness, but it is sadder still to think that when He gives us a second, third, or sometimes a tenth opportunity we still fail to grasp the opportunity. It is time for us to wake up to the realization that the only reason Jesus does not come this very moment is that we might have another opportunity to help another to be prepared for His coming. This thought should put an urgency into our efforts at evangelism which we may not have felt before.

Second, the delay in His coming means that all sinners are given another opportunity to be saved. Instead of mocking, those critics of the first century should have expressed gratitude that the Lord had delayed His coming. This delay could mean their salvation. A little later in this same chapter Peter urges his readers to "account that the long-suffering of our Lord is salvation" (v. 15).

When Jesus comes again to earth there will be no more evangelistic appeal; therefore, every day that He delays His coming is an additional day of grace. He has delayed His coming until now, but we cannot guarantee that He will delay it any longer.

We can only assume that He has delayed it until this moment in order that the unsaved person might have this one more opportunity to receive Him as Savior, so that when He does come he may welcome His coming with joy and not have to seek hiding under some rock, trying to escape the fury of His final judgment. We cannot tell the unbeliever how much longer He will delay, but we can tell him that Jesus has delayed until this present hour because He loves him and wants him to have His wonderful redemption.

12
THE PROSPECT OF THE SECOND COMING

Even though the second coming of Christ has been delayed much longer than the early Christians thought that it would, the prospect of His return has in no wise been abandoned. After explaining to his readers the reason for the delay, the apostle Peter proceeds to reiterate his confidence in Christ's return to earth. Though He has not yet come, He will come, and when He does come it will be as a thief in the night.

He will come when the world least expects Him to come. His business will not be the same as that of a thief, but He will come as a thief in the sense that He will come when people least expect Him. This is the third time that we find that word, "thief," used in connection with the second coming of Christ. Jesus Himself used it in His address to His disciples on Mount Olivet (Matt. 14:43-44). The apostle Paul also used it in his First Letter to the Thessalonians (5:2).

After reiterating the certainty of His coming, Peter goes on to show what effect this anticipation should have on those who believe in it. These are his words:

> But the day of the Lord will come as a thief in the night; in which the heavens shall pass away with a great noise, and the elements shall melt with fervent heat, the earth also and the works that are therein shall be burned up. Seeing then that all these things shall be dissolved, what manner of persons ought ye to be in all holy conversation and godliness, looking for and hasting unto the coming

of the day of God, wherein the heavens being on fire shall be dissolved, and the elements shall melt with fervent heat? Nevertheless, we, according to his promise, look for new heavens and a new earth, wherein dwelleth righteousness. Wherefore, beloved, seeing that ye look for such things, be diligent that ye may be found of him in peace, without spot, and blameless (3:10-14).

In this paragraph Peter reveals some of the issues related to the return of Christ to earth, but our examination of these will be reserved for the next chapter. In this chapter we are concerned with what Peter wrote about the effect upon Christians of the prospect of this return of Christ.

The Certainty of Its Prospect

Three times in this one brief paragraph Peter uses the word, "expect," giving emphasis to his confidence in the return of Christ. The Christians of the first century looked expectantly for the coming of Christ. The return of Christ loomed large in their prospect for the future. In this respect the first-century Christians were different from twentieth-century Christians. The average present-day Christian seldom thinks in terms of the prospect of Christ's second coming. Dr. Perry F. Webb has given a vivid description of this difference in these words:

> The early Christians had a spirit of expectancy which we do not possess. They had a hope which we have largely lost. Their lives were marked by an attitude of anticipation to which we are largely strangers. They expected, anticipated, and longed for the return of the Lord. We seldom think of His return and as for living in constant expectation of it, we simply do not.[1]

But we have the same promises which they had and the same scripture upon which to base our anticipation of His coming.

Some might doubt the idea of the second coming of Christ to earth, but no one can doubt that the Scriptures prophesy it. There are literally hundreds of references in the New Testament to the second coming of Christ to earth. Here are only a few samples from these many scripture passages: Luke 2:8; Acts 1:11; Phil. 3:20; James 5:7; Heb. 9:27, 28; 1 Thess. 4:12-15; John 14:1-3; 1 Cor. 11:26. We have just as much reason as the early Christians to live in the conscious prospect of the return of Christ to earth. In spite of the fact that He has delayed His coming for these 2,000 years, it is still a certified fact that Jesus is coming again, certified by the irrevocable promises of God as given in His infallible and authoritative Word.

The Effect of Its Prospect

Living in the prospect of the second coming has its effect upon our life here and now. Every expectation concerning the future has its effect upon one's attitude and conduct in the present. The anticipation of something important in the future cannot be looked at with a purely academic mind. It will inevitably have its impact upon one's present feeling and attitude. Many discourage anything that speaks of hope for the future because, as they claim, it has no relation to the needs of the present hour. These contend that what we need is not "pie in the sky by and by," but a sincere and successful encounter with the problems of the here and now.

But those who hold this position are sadly mistaken in thinking that hope for the future has no effect upon the problems of the present. The fact is that hope for the future is indispensable in coping with the problems of the present. Without it the present becomes meaningless and despairing. George Adam Smith had a sermon in which he discussed the "Moral Meaning of Hope."[2] Basing his thought on the words of the apostle Peter in this third chapter of his Second Epistle, Dr. Smith pointed out that hope has a two-fold effect in the moral realm. It stimulates conscience and produces character. Hope rouses conscience and inspires noble character. We do not mean to give the idea that just any kind of hope will do this, but hope in the return of Christ to this earth will do it. This, in essence, is what Peter is conveying in this passage. For those who believe, the prospect of Christ's second coming should do at least four things.

First, this prospect should stimulate within us a desire for purity of moral character. "Wherefore, beloved, seeing that ye look for such things, be diligent that ye may be found of him in peace, without spot, and blameless" (v. 14). Knowing that He will suddenly appear before us in glory stirs within the Christian a desire to be pure as He is pure. We shudder at the thought of His coming to find us covered with the impurities of this world. Peter tells us that we should strive to be without spot and without blame. These are two words Peter used together on three occasions in his two Epistles. He tells us in his First Epistle that Christ "was without spot and without blame" when he offered Himself as our atonement (1 Pet 1:19). The very same two words are used here as in the paragraph we are now considering.

Then in describing the false teachers in the second chapter of his Second Epistle, the apostle writes that they are "spots and blemishes." Here again we have the same two words without the negative prefixes. The false religionists are full of impurities and blemishes, but the true believers, in anticipation of His return, seek to present themselves before Him without spot or blemish. For the true Christian there are many incentives for purity of life, but there is no incentive quite so strong as that which comes from thoughts of His imminent return to earth. The apostle John expressed this same idea in his First Epistle: "Beloved, now are we the sons of God, and it doth not yet appear what we shall be: but we know that, when he shall appear, we shall be like him; for we shall see him as he is. And every man that hath this hope in him purifieth himself, even as he is pure" (1 John 3:2-3).

I may have any number of reasons for wanting to keep my character pure, but the reason which looms most prominent in my mind is the thought of being able to stand before Him when He comes in His glory without the shame of a blemished character.

Once a young man who was serving overseas in the army was invited by his buddies to go with them to a nearby town for a night of indulgence in licentiousness. He declined with the explanation that he was expecting to return soon to a waiting bride in the states, and he wanted to give to her a spotless character because she was worthy of the best. In some such way the Christian wants to present to His Lord at His coming a character which has not been besmirched with the filth of this world.

Second, the prospect of His coming inspires a more complete dedication to God in a life of reverence and respect. Listen again to Peter's appeal: "Seeing then that all these things shall be dissolved, what manner of persons ought ye to be in all holy conversation and godliness?" (v. 11). In the light of the prospect of His coming we should seek to maintain a "holy conversation and godliness." "Conversation" might be better translated by the words, "manner of life." To have a "holy" manner of life is to have a life separated unto the will of God.

"Godliness" carries the idea of reverence and respect for God. It is not enough merely to keep our characters morally clean. The true Christian will also want to live a life of reverence, that is, he will want to respect God in the sense of doing His will and dedicating himself to that way of life to which God has called him. This desire will be intensified by the consciousness of our Savior's return to earth.

Third, the prospect of His return should stir up within us a desire to be at peace with ourselves and with others. Peter admonished his readers, in the light of the promise of Christ's return, to give diligence "that ye may be found of him in peace" (v. 14). We would not want the Lord to come and find us bickering with our fellow men. We cannot help it if men hate us because we dare to stand for that which is right and Christlike, but there is no excuse for personal bickering and feuding.

Paul said, "as much as lieth in you, be at peace with all men" (Rom. 12:18). This injunction takes on much more meaning and urgency when we think of the promised coming of Christ to earth again. There is little we can do to stop wars and rumors of wars in our world of selfishness and greed, but there is much we can do to maintain peace in our personal relations with others, especially with other Christians. Christians can more easily forget their differences and forgive one another when they live in the consciousness of the imminent return of Christ.

Fourth, the prospect of Christ's return should stir up within us a sense of anxious expectancy. This is the missing note in twentieth-century Christianity. If we believe that Christ is coming again in glory to consummate His kingdom, then we should anxiously live in the expectation of it. Three times Peter uses this word in verses 12 through 14, once in each verse. It is translated in the *King James Version* as "looking for." In verse 12 it is "looking for and hasting unto the coming of the day of God." In verse 13 we find, "nevertheless, we, according to his promise, look for new heavens and a new earth." In verse 14 we read, "wherefore, beloved, seeing that ye look for such things."

It was the predominant attitude of all the Christians of the first century—a certain eager anticipation for the appearing of the Lord. Peter intensifies this idea of expectation in verse 12 by adding the word, "hasting." In a sermon that appeared in the September 28, 1962, issue of *Christianity Today*, A. Skevington Wood explains the meaning of this additional word in this manner:

> Christians are not only looking for but hasting unto the coming of God's great day. That does not mean, as the *Revised Version* margin suggests, that they are hastening the arrival of the end, for no man can do that. The times and the seasons are altogether in the hand of God, and nothing we do can either advance or retard them. What the apostle tells us here is that believers are hastening towards that day with eager desire and fervent longing. They are running a race, and this is the goal always in view.[3]

The Thrill of Its Prospect

Even though many modern-day Christians have lost this eagerness of expectation, when we stop long enough to ponder the reality and significance of the second coming as revealed in the Holy Scriptures, there will surely rise up within us a thrill of ecstasy at the very thought of it. We have lost the eagerness of anticipation only because we have neglected the teaching of the Word of God on it. We need a revival of eager expectancy as it was manifested in the hearts of these first-century Christians. Such a spirit of expectancy will bring back some of the thrill of Christian living.

There are many thrills in the Christian way of life, but there is no thrill quite so exhilarating as the thought of our Lord's return. This is not something reserved for idle dreamers who live in another world and have little interest or contact with the present problems of our turbulent existence here. It is a thrill that makes the present more meaningful and fruitful. With the words of the late C. S. Lewis in his book, *Christian Behaviour*, let us close this meditation:

> Hope is one of the theological virtues. This means that a continual looking forward to the eternal world is not (as some modern people think) a form of escapism or wishful thinking, but one of the things a Christian is meant to do. It does not mean that we are to leave the present world as it is. If you read history you will find that the Christians who did most for the present world were just those who thought most of the next. . . . It is since Christians have largely ceased to think of the other world that they have become so ineffective in this. Aim at heaven and you will get earth thrown in; aim at earth and you will get neither.[4]

13
THE ISSUES OF THE SECOND COMING

In 2 Peter 3, Simon Peter not only discusses the delay of the second coming of Christ and its effect upon our attitude and conduct, but also the events related to that event. The return of Christ, according to Peter, would issue in certain significant events.

Let us remind the reader in beginning that there are other factors related to the second coming that are not mentioned in Peter's discourse here. These other issues will come in for consideration as we examine other passages of scripture in this study. Here we are dealing only with those mentioned by Peter in this third chapter.

Peter, it seems, was not concerned about any order of events or any dividing up of the events into stages. He does mention three issues involved in the second coming. We shall consider them as they are presented by the apostle in this text without trying to fit them into any kind of an eschatological and chronological order.

The Dissolution of This Earth

The first thing which attracts our attention in Peter's description of the second coming is the dissolution of this earth. The second coming will bring to an end this present world order. The principal subject running through this whole chapter is the second coming of Christ; therefore, everything in it relates to and is associated with the event. In describing this wonderful event Peter gives this explanation:

> But the day of the Lord will come as a thief in the night; in which the heavens shall pass away with a great noise, and the elements shall melt with fervent heat, the earth also and the works that are therein shall be burned up... Looking for and hasting unto the coming of the day of God, wherein the heavens being on fire shall be dissolved, and the elements shall melt with fervent heat (3:10, 12).

The coming of Christ will issue in a great and terrible day. Peter had explained earlier in this chapter that the old world was destroyed by water, but that the present world is being reserved for a judgment of fire. Whether or not Peter is giving to us here a literal picture of the end of this world we are not sure. But whether it is literal or figurative it does definitely prophesy the dissolution of this present world order.

Some have suggested that God might use the tools of man's own making to accomplish this dissolution. We would not be dogmatic at this point, but this could well be the case. We are developing unbelievable firepower through nuclear science. Scientists have been telling us for some time that another war on a worldwide scale could easily destroy all habitation on this earth in a few days. Could this be God's means of bringing fulfillment to Peter's prophecy in our text?

Whether it is or isn't, we can rest assured that when Jesus comes again, this earth on which we live will be consumed and destroyed. This earth was created by God's own hand, but it was not destined to be eternal. The prophet Joel describes this great day of the coming of the Lord with these words: "The sun shall be turned into darkness, and the moon into blood, before the great and the terrible day of the Lord come" (Joel 2:31). From the Isle of Patmos the apostle John described this great day of destruction in vividly dramatic figures of seven bowls of wrath. We will have occasion to look at these in a subsequent chapter.

As Dr. Ray Summers explains, "It is the divine purpose that the present order shall not stand forever. There is to be a complete change. Whether or not the things mentioned here are literal is not known. It is extremely doubtful if this passage should be made the basis for any cosmological program for the end of time."[1] Whatever else Peter may have meant by this reference it is certain that he did not believe in the eternality of matter as did Plato and some modern materialists. As God once destroyed the world by flood, so He can destroy it again by fire. He holds the universe in His hands. He created it by His word, and He can destroy it the same way.

It is interesting to note that some scientists do recognize the possibility and even the probability of the dissolution of the world. In a *Journal of Christian Philosophy*, Professor Alexander Winchell makes the following interesting comment:

> Our earth is approaching a finality through various causes of change. Its surface is wearing out, and its lands becoming sea-sediments. Its progressive refrigeration will result in the complete absorption of atmosphere and water. Tidal action will slacken the rate of rotation until each side is turned alternately two weeks toward the scorching sun, and the two weeks toward the cold regions of space. If this is not enough, the sun is destined to be extinguished, and the earth to be precipitated upon the central funeral pile of our system. Any one of these contingencies demonstrates that the duration of the habitable globe is limited.[2]

There is evidence of deterioration in our earth now, in spite of all efforts of conservation and development. This should be a sign to all that our earth is marked for destruction. This utter dissolution will come to pass in connection with the return of our Lord. We often act as if we believed that this earth would stand forever and that we ourselves would remain on it forever, but we are wrong on both scores. Most of us will admit, when we are brought face to face with it, that we will not remain on this earth forever, but few people really recognize the ephemeral nature of the earth itself. According to the Scriptures this last fact is as certain as the first one.

The Judgment of the Wicked

Not only will the earth itself be dissolved when Jesus comes again, but there will also come a fearful judgment upon the wicked who live or have lived upon it. Peter brings this out in verse 7: "But the heavens and the earth, which are now, by the same word are kept in store, reserved unto fire against the day of judgment and perdition of ungodly men." The apostle does not give us a detailed description of this judgment. He only states the fact, but just to mention that it will involve judgment and perdition makes it tragic enough.

Whether this judgment will take place twenty-five seconds after the appearing of Christ or seven years makes little difference. The time element is inconsequential. What *is* of mammoth consequence is the fact that the coming of Christ to earth will issue in a final judgment upon all who have not recognized God in Christ. There is a sense in which the unbeliever receives the judgment of hell at the moment of his death, but at the coming of Christ there will be a resurrection of the wicked, as well as of the believer.

At this time there will be an official and public consignment of the wicked to the eternal abode of torment. This is corroborated by the words of Jesus as recorded by John: "Marvel not at this: for the hour is coming in which all that are in the graves shall hear his voice. And shall come forth; they that have done good, unto the resurrection of life; and they that have done evil, unto the resurrection of damnation" (5:28-29).

Some insist that this is a reference to two separate judgments separated by a space of time (seven years), but there is nothing in this particular passage to suggest two separate judgments, much less a period of time in between. What Jesus seems to be saying is simply this: At the time of His return to the earth there will be a resurrection of all the dead, that is, the bodies of all persons who have been buried in the earth will come forth. This resurrection will not mean the same thing to all people. To some it will mean the beginning of a glorious bodily existence in heaven; to others it will mean the beginning of a bodily existence in eternal torment. To make it mean more than this is to read into the text that which is not there.

In 2 Peter 3 we have no indication of any such distinction. We have only the simple reminder that the coming of Christ to earth will issue in the great day of terrible judgment for the unbelievers. In that day they will stand before the just Judge to receive a just sentence, and all of it will take place in connection with the return of Christ.

The Creation of a New Earth

Another interesting issue growing out of the return of Christ will be the creation of new heavens and a new earth. Peter also makes this crystal clear: "Nevertheless we, according to his promise, look for new heavens and a new earth, wherein dwelleth righteousness" (v. 13). Peter has nothing in his Epistle about a millennium in which the saints will reign with Christ on earth. This is not to say anything either for or against the idea of a millennial reign of Christ on earth. We only note in passing that Peter writes nothing about it. We will consider this aspect of it when we come to the passage in the twentieth chapter of the Revelation.

Peter does assert that in connection with the second coming of Christ there will be the dissolution of this present earth and the creation of a new earth. The word "new" here carries the idea of a different kind. The new heavens and earth will not be just another version of the present ones. It will be more than a program of remodeling. God will completely destroy the present heavens and earth and bring into existence a completely new kind.

We do not know what the difference will be from the standpoint of substance. The Bible has not revealed to us these technical details, but it does describe for us one very important difference. Peter tells us that this new earth will be a place "wherein dwelleth righteousness." Our present world is full of corruption and sin. The evidences are ample on every hand. But when Jesus comes again He will destroy this earth which is full of corruption by evil men and will bring into existence a new earth which will be free from the contamination of sin. On it only those who have been redeemed from the guilt and dominion of sin will be permitted to live. It will be a kingdom of righteousness.

It matters little where this new earth will be from the standpoint of location in God's great universe. Some seem to think that it will be in the same location as this present one. This is a possibility, but it is useless to argue the point. The important fact to remember is that it will be characterized by righteousness rather than sin. Being a habitation of the righteous it will be a place of beauty and magnificent symmetry. It will be without sin; therefore, it will be a place without suffering, hate, oppression, poverty, or death. This is another way of stating that it will be heaven.

There is bound to be a delightful place to which the souls of the redeemed go who die before the Lord comes again. But God is doubtlessly preparing to create a wonderful new place of exquisite beauty and glory out of the ruins of this old world in which we now live. And when the Savior comes again He will resurrect these dead bodies to be reunited with their redeemed souls and to be placed on this new and eternal abode of the saints called "new heavens and a new earth." What a blessed day that will be for those who have been redeemed in the precious blood of Christ!

The coming of Christ to earth again will doubtlessly mean even more than this, but according to Peter in 2 Peter 3, it will bring to pass three momentous events: the dissolution of this earth; the final judgment upon the wicked; and the creation of new heavens and a new earth as a habitation of the redeemed. How remarkably similar is this eschatological picture of Peter to that painted by Jesus in Matthew 24 and 25!

PART IV
THE ESCHATOLOGY OF JOHN

14
THE LAST HOUR

In the five books of the New Testament attributed to John the apostle there are a number of allusions to the return of Christ and the end of the age, but there are two passages which seem to deal directly and in some detail with the subject of eschatology. One is found in 1 John 2, and the other in the last half of the Apocalypse. Here we are concerned with the passage in 1 John. The passage reads as follows:

> Little children, it is the last time; and as ye have heard that antichrist shall come, even now are there many antichrists; whereby we know that it is the last time. They went out from us, but they were not of us; for if they had been of us, they would no doubt have continued with us; but they went out, that they might be made manifest that they were not all of us. But ye have an unction from the Holy One, and ye know all things (2:18, 19).

In these verses two things intrigue us—his reference to the last time and to the antichrist. Since the days of the prophets there has been a prevalent feeling among religious leaders that the end of the world would be preceded by the appearance of some great anti-God movement or person. These two subjects, therefore, are always related. In developing the thought suggested in this text we shall raise four questions for our consideration: (1) What is meant by "the last time?" (2) What are the evidences of the last time? (3) Who is the antichrist? And (4) What is the meaning of all this for us?

The Last Time

John tells his readers that "it is the last time." Actually the word which John uses here is "hour" instead of "time," and there is no article preceding the word. A more literal rendering, therefore, would make it read like this: "It is a last hour." Some have made much of the anarthrous use of the word, hour, indicating that it must have had some special significance for the apostle. Others think that it is the same as if he had used the article since it was customary to omit the article with familiar terms.

According to the former, the omitting of the article tones down the assertion. Dr. W. T. Conner is one of these who notes the omission of the article and interprets John to say that the present hour has the characteristics of a last hour, not that it literally is *the* last hour.[1]

Others tone it down by saying that John had reference here to the last era in world history, the Christian dispensation. According to this theory the whole period of Christian history constitutes the last hour of world history. Henry A. Sawtelle, in *The American Commentary*, so interprets the mind of the apostle here. He explains that the last hour is "the last stage of the world's religious history. There is to be no other season of salvation, no added forces of redemption in some after era. . . . This is the last dispensation, the great ingatherings of Gentiles or Jews are to take place in it, and not beyond it."[2]

Either one of these two interpretations might be true, but I cannot help but feel that the apostle John had more than this in mind. I have the impression that he was thinking of the imminence of the actual end of the world and the second coming of Christ. John nowhere in this Epistle speaks directly of the return of Christ to earth, but it is implied here and elsewhere. A. Plummer calls our attention to the fact that "the last day" is a phrase peculiar to John and invariably means the end of the world.[3] Even though the article does not appear in the Greek, there are good reasons for believing that the expression is nevertheless definite, and is rightfully rendered in the English with the article, "the last hour."

Some students of the scripture are reluctant to make this expression refer to the end of the world in order to protect John from what might appear to be a glaring mistake. If John, writing under inspiration, believed that the end of the world was really imminent, how is it that nearly 2,000 years have passed and still no end? Did John really make a mistake in his calculations? The best answer to this question has been given by the gifted New Testament scholar, H. E. Dana, in these words:

> Every state in the historical development of redemption is now in the past except one—the triumphant return of Christ. Therefore the end abides as the potential fact ever right over against us, and more imminently so in times of great stress and peril. We cannot justly accuse John of a "mistake" where he is but giving expression to a natural and rightful reaction of Christian consciousness.[4]

No Christian is ever wrong in any generation to look upon any hour as the last hour, for it could well be. Every hour in our present world experience is a potential last hour. Instead of accusing John of a mistake, we would all be closer to the New Testament truth and attitude if we looked upon our hour as the last hour. Furthermore, in God's sight and in the light of eternity, a day may be as a thousand years or a thousand years as a day, as Peter explains in his Second Epistle.

Evidences of the Last Hour

John's statement concerning the last hour was not some rash assertion that had no basis or justification. John had good reason to believe that it was the last hour, even as we have good reason to believe that we are living in the last days. The primary reason for believing this is the presence of the antichrist. "As ye have heard that antichrist shall come, even now are there many antichrists; whereby we know that it is the last time."

Just as the prophets of the Old Testament believed that the appearing of the Messiah on earth would be preceded by some outstanding opposition to God, so the New Testament apostles believed that the second appearing of Christ on earth would be preceded by a demonstration of antichrist. The term antichrist appears only here and in 2 John; however, the idea of an arch-opponent to Christ is present in both testaments. The word itself has two possible meanings. It could mean someone who appears in the stead of Christ, someone who takes His place, or it could mean someone who stands against Christ. The first idea implies also the second. He who takes His place is against Him.

As explained by Charles A. Briggs in the *New Schaff-Herzog Religious Encyclopedia*, "the idea of antichrist is in earlier New Testament writings, and its roots are in the Old Testament. . . . Gradually the last enemy of the kingdom of God came to be thought of as the antitype of the Messiah."[5]

In the seventh and eighth chapters of the prophecy of Daniel we find references to the appearing of a great arch-opponent of the Messiah. It is possible that Daniel was thinking of the time just before the end of the world, or it could be he was thinking of the final enemy of God to appear before the coming of the Messiah the first time. If this be true, Antiochus Epiphanes IV fits into the picture appropriately. In either case it is the idea of the appearing of an arch-opponent before the coming of the Messiah, whether at His first advent or His second.

The New Testament alludes frequently to the appearing of such an antichrist before the return of Christ, though he is not called by this particular name except in the Epistles of John. Jesus Himself warned His disciples of false Christs who will come just before the end and seek to deceive even the elect (Matt. 24:24). Paul describes this antichrist who shall appear just before the end as "the man of sin" and "the mystery of lawlessness" (2 Thess. 2). There is much that is parallel in John's description of the antichrist and Paul's description of the man of sin. They must have had the same thing in mind.

The appearance of such an arch-opponent is a sure sign of the imminence of the return of our Lord and the dissolution of this world. John knew the end was near because of the presence of the antichrist; even so, we may know that the end is near by the presence of such an antichrist.

Identity of the antichrist

Students of the Bible, history, and religion have identified the antichrist with many different personalities and movements. Questions such as these cry out for an answer: Is he a person, persons, or a principle? Is he one or many? What are his chief characteristics? From whence does he come? To some of these questions we cannot give a dogmatic answer, but we shall try to answer these questions as nearly as we can, according to the information John gives us in our text.

As to whether he is a person, persons, or a principle, we might answer, "He is all three." John reminds his readers that they had heard of the coming of antichrist (singular). He may have had reference to Paul's "man of sin" here. If so, he was a person, and yet both Paul and John seem to suggest that this antichrist represents a principle of unbelief or blasphemy. John does not refute the report that the antichirst would come; he simply adds the fact that many antichrists had already come. In this sense the antichrist is plural. There is also a sense in which antichrist is an attitude that denies Jesus as the Christ. Wherever such an attitude prevails there is antichrist, but there is another sense in which antichrist is a person, for one cannot separate an attitude from a person. Only persons have attitudes. Anyone who expresses the attitude described above is antichrist. In this sense, therefore, there are many antichrists.

There is still another sense in which the Bible seems to expect the appearing, close to the time of Christ's return, of one who will be the expressive personification of all unbelief and rebellion.

John does not dwell on this aspect of it, but neither does he deny it. Though he does not refer to him by the name antichrist, John does seem to think in terms of one outstanding personal leader of the combined forces of unrighteousness when he mentions the "beast" in his Apocalypse. And Paul's "man of sin" seems to be a reference to a particular individual who will rise up in the last days with mighty power.

Speculation has been rife among Bible students with reference to the identity of this personal antichrist. In the early days of the Christian movement from the political point of view this antichrist was identified with Nero, who, according to legend, would reappear in resurrected form to continue his terrible reign. A little later Domitian seemed to be the most likely candidate for the title of antichrist. Thus through the centuries many different political leaders have been identified as the antichrist. Luther and Calvin identified him with the pope, but the pope, in turn, classified the Reformation leaders as the personification of antichrist.

It may be there will yet be one person to appear who will fit exactly the pattern of the antichrist. Such a supposition is not completely without any biblical basis. If and when such an individual does appear, he will be the ring leader of a thousand other little antichrists. Perhaps we should place our emphasis, not upon the appearing of a singular individual whom we shall seek to identify, but upon the principle which is expressed by such an antichrist, a principle which is evident in the lives of many people already living among us.

From John's description we learn that the antichrist is anyone who denies that Jesus is the Christ. One may believe that Jesus lived, that He accomplished great things, and that God exists and is sovereign, but if he does not identify the Jesus of Nazareth with the Christ, the Anointed One of God, he has denied the fundamental truth of the Christian faith and may on this basis be classified as antichrist. We must identify the human Jesus with the divine Christ in our belief.

One does not have to be an out-and-out atheist or infidel in order to be antichrist. The fact is that these antichrists come out from among those who call themselves Christians. The antichrist is one who has an association with the Christian movement. The arch-opponent of Christ will come from among those who call themselves Christians, not from the ranks of atheists. They will emerge from among these Christians because they were never a vital part of the Christian community in the first place. This John explains in these words: "They went out from us, but they were not of us; for if they had been of us, they would no doubt have continued with us: but they went out, that they might be made manifest that they were not all of us" (v. 19).

It is not the case of a Christian who apostasizes. The very fact that one apparently apostasizes is proof that he was never a genuine part of the Christian community. It is possible for one to be identified with the Christian movement and yet never acknowledge Jesus as the Christ and Lord of his life. Whenever one claims for himself the power to absolve sin, is he not taking the place of Christ? This is antichrist.

The Meaning for Us

There is little to be gained by a lengthy argument on the identity of the antichrist or the meaning of the last times. There are, however, some vital lessons here for all of us. Three facts should be understood from this discussion of the antichrist.

First, we should understand that the forces of evil and ungodliness are already at work in our world. We need not wait until some future date to see the evidences of the work of the antichrist. As John explained, already there are many antichrists.

Second, it should be understood that those who are not genuinely anchored to Christ will be deceived and will fall away. Many so-called Christians will turn away from the Christian faith in the last days, but not one genuine Christian will be caught in this exodus.

Third, let every Christian be assured that these forces of evil, whether in principle or in person, will be finally destroyed forever at the coming of Christ. John implies that the final victory will be won by those who in truth and sincerity have received Jesus Christ as Lord of their lives, even though they may be in the minority. God has vouchsafed this victory to His redeemed children. John declares this plainly in 1 John 4:4—"Ye are of God, little children, and have overcome them; because greater is he that is in you, than he that is in the world."

15
ESCHATOLOGY IN THE APOCALYPSE

In the minds of most Christians eschatology is associated with the Book of Revelation. In fact, most of them believe that the whole book is basically eschatological and deals almost exclusively with the doctrine of last things. That the Apocalypse has something to say about eschatology no one can deny; however, it may not reveal as much on the subject as some Bible scholars seem to think it does.

One's approach to the Apocalypse has much to do with what one finds in it on the subject of eschatology. Some, for instance, have taken the "preterist" attitude which looks upon the Book as a series of oracles or events having only historical significance. To these the book has nothing to do with the present or the future. It is simply a historical document which refers to the Christians of the first century. To them it is interesting and valuable from the standpoint of history but has no real pertinent value as a revelation of what will happen in the future. According to this attitude there is nothing eschatological in the Book.

There are others who take the attitude that in the Book of Revelation we have a panoramic view of world history, or, at least, Christian history. These find a prophetic reference to every major event in history, plus events which are yet to be. These, of course, do find some eschatological value in the Book.

Then there is the "futurist" who assumes that everything in the Book is eschatological, that is, in the main body of the Book (chapters 4 through 22). Most futurists assume the position that most, if not all of the Book, reveals events that will occur during the seven years of tribulation just before the return of Christ.

A fourth approach is known as the "philosophy-of-history attitude." Those who take this attitude look upon the Book of Revelation as a purely symbolic representation of the philosophical factors of history. They see no particular events as such revealed in the Book, but only some symbols of historical philosophy. These, of course, find no eschatological value in the Book.

Perhaps some aspects of each of these attitudes ought to be incorporated into our thinking as we approach a study of the Apocalypse. We would suggest there is real historical value to be found in it, plus the recurrence of some great historical principles which may be applied to any era of history, but there is also a prophetic element that points to the future. I see the Book of Revelation as a panoramic view of God's redemptive plan and program, from its inception to its glorious consummation. It is a picture of the unfolding drama of redemption as it is seen from heaven's point of view and reveals all that God has done, is doing, and will do in utterly defeating and destroying the forces of evil and giving glorious and complete victory to His own redeemed people. John simply records what he sees through that open door into heaven.

According to what John reveals in this picture there are seven major episodes in this drama of redemption. They are unfolded before us in logical order but not necessarily in chronological order. So far as time is concerned many of them overlap; however, the last three are definitely future. The seven episodes are as follows:

1. A picture of a sovereign and majestic God sitting on a throne (4:1-5:14).

2. A picture of righteous judgments coming from this sovereign God and the Lamb (6:1-8:5).

3. A picture of timely and forceful warning from this sovereign God (8:6-11:19).

4. A picture of the inevitable conflict between the forces of evil and the forces of righteousness (12:1-15:8).

5. A picture of the climax of this conflict (16).

6. A picture of the celebration of victory (17:1-20:10).

7. A picture of eternal destiny (20:11-22:5).

For our purposes here we will pass over the first four of these and concentrate on the last three, particularly the fifth and sixth since the seventh deals with eternal destiny, that is, the state of being beyond the last things. For further study of the whole book the reader is referred to the author's book, *Revelation: Book of Mystery and Hope*, published by Broadman in 1979.

A conflict is now being waged, and has been since the days of Adam and Eve, between the forces of evil in the world and the forces of righteousness, but there will come a time, yet future, when this conflict will reach a climax. Just when this will be no one knows but God; however, John is given a symbolic preview of this climax and he describes it for us in the sixteenth chapter of his Apocalypse. It is the time when He will empty His seven bowls of wrath upon the armies of the wicked.

A time is coming in the history of redemption when God will say "it is enough." Then He will put forth His "Sunday punch," even as our nation did during the war with Japan. After four years of skirmishes with the Japanese in the South Sea Islands, in which the war went back and forth, our president and military leaders came together and decided it was time for our last resort, the atomic bomb. Soon, in 1945, the bombs were dropped on two major cities in Japan, and that was the end of the war. So it shall be in the end time. God has a "nuclear bomb" ready to be dropped on the enemies of righteousness in the form of seven bowls of wrath. The time will come when God will command His angels to empty these bowls of wrath on the kingdom of Satan. When that occurs the war will be over.

As John describes this scene from the portals of heaven, the reader can see the reeling and rocking of the soldiers in Satan's army. The first four bowls involve the elements of nature—earth, sea, rivers, and sky. The fifth falls directly on the kingdom of the beast. The sixth releases the armies from the East. As Satan begins to see the handwriting on the wall, he does what any commanding general would do in time of conflict. He prepares to make one more all-out, last-ditch stand, hoping to turn the tide of battle.

The last-ditch effort of Satan to turn the tide of battle is pictured in this sixteenth chapter of Revelation as the battle of Armageddon. Some have interpreted this battle of Armageddon as a literal war to be fought with the usual instruments of warfare in the land of Israel during the seven-year period of tribulation at the end of the age. That it does have reference to a decisive struggle at the end of the age we cannot deny, but to claim that it will be a literal earthly warfare at some particular spot is reading into the text more than was intended.

The whole picture is couched in figurative language, designed to be symbolic. The armies of Satan for this decisive battle are to be recruited by three slick, slimy frogs which come up out of the mouth of the dragon. No one has ever suggested that this will be literally fulfilled. Every one recognizes that this is a symbolic picture, and yet many will insist that the reference to Armageddon will be literally fulfilled. Both references are found in the same figurative context. Consistency requires that both be interpreted as symbolic or both literal. The former makes more sense.

Armageddon is a word that John coined. It literally means "the mount of Megiddo." The term "Megiddo" appears in the Old Testament and refers to a narrow strip of plain just South of Nazareth in Palestine. There is a mount overlooking this valley, which was also called the Plain of Esdraelon. On this little mound can be seen the ruins of the ancient city of Megiddo. Many of the most decisive battles of Israel's history were fought in this plain; therefore, through the years this plain became in the minds of the Jews a symbol of conflict or decisive battle. John uses the word here in the same sense.

This is the idea: When God begins to pour out the fullness of His fury on the forces of evil, Satan is going to rally his forces for one last immense effort to turn the tide of battle, but exactly when he thinks he is making some progress, that seventh angel is going to step forward with the most powerful "atomic bomb." Then will we hear the voice from heaven calling out, "It is done." The battle is over; the victory is won.

For this writer or any other to predict the time of this climactic event would be rank presumption. We only know that it will happen at the end of the age and in connection with the return of Christ. All of this corresponds with the other New Testament teachings concerning the great period of tribulation directly before the return of Christ. However, we have yet to find any scriptural, undeniable proof that it will be a literal period of seven years.

After this climactic battle and after the last bowl of wrath has been emptied out on the wicked kingdom of Satan, there will be a tremendous celebration of victory. This celebration will contain a number of features. The first will be a tour of the battlefield to see the utter devastation of this evil kingdom, especially the seat of Satan's kingdom, symbolized by the ancient term, Babylon, long a symbol of evil's headquarters. The saints will rejoice and shout for joy as they see the ruins of the once-mighty enemy of righteousness (Rev. 17-18).

This will be followed by three heavenly scenes of celebration. The first will be a victory concert by the heavenly choir, made up of redeemed saints and angels. They will sing a "Hallelujah Chorus" with words such as these: "Alleluia; Salvation, and glory, and honour, and power, unto the Lord our God: For true and righteous are his judgments" (Rev. 19:1-2). Then will follow the magnificent wedding of the ages when the Lamb shall be married to His Bride for eternity. The Bride will be the Church, the total body of all the truly redeemed of all ages. This is the real Church, the heavenly Bride of Christ. The Groom will be dressed in His robes of royalty. The Bride will be bedecked in her gown of pure and spotless white. No wedding on earth can compare with it from the standpoint of sheer beauty, pomp, and majesty. Now we are betrothed to Christ; at the end of the age when the conflict is over, we shall be joined to Christ in the intimacy of spiritual marriage for eternity (Rev. 19:7-10).

The third event in this heavenly celebration will be a stately and colorful triumphant procession through the streets of the New Jerusalem. Leading the parade will be none other than the Lord Jesus Himself, riding on a beautiful white horse, robed in royalty with a sharp sword protruding out of His mouth and these words across His vesture: "King of kings and Lord of lords." Riding behind Him will be unnumbered redeemed saints on white horses and wearing white garments. What a contrast to the so-called "triumphal entry" of Jesus into Jerusalem as recorded by Matthew in chapter 21 of his Gospel! Then He rode on a lowly ass clothed in the rags of poverty. A few spread their palm leaves along the route and shouted "Hosanna, to the Son of David: blessed is he that cometh in the name of the Lord: Hosanna in the highest" (Matt. 21:9). But most of them stood by to criticize and vilify. In this magnificent procession at the end of the age He will bask in the praise and honor of all the redeemed in heaven (Rev. 19:11-16).

Another feature of the celebration will be the privilege of witnessing the official consignment of the wicked leaders into the lake of fire (Rev. 19:17-21). We look rejoicingly with John as the beast and the false prophet are cast into a lake of fire burning with brimstone.

Every feature of the celebration will be significant, but there is one special feature that will be extremely fascinating and delightful to all the redeemed. That special feature is described for us in the first six verses of chapter 20, a passage which has been variously interpreted by Bible scholars through the years. In fact, on this passage alone thousands of volumes have been written. Many of them seem to have found in this passage the biblical basis for an elaborate and complicated doctrine known as "millennialism." This is derived from the Latin word for "thousand" and was suggested by the reference to a thousand years in this passage. The only reference in the entire Bible to a thousand-year reign is in this one highly figurative passage. It is somewhat strange that many highly regarded Bible scholars who recognize the figurative and symbolic nature of the language of the Revelation will come to this one little passage and insist that it must be interpreted literally, signaling the coming of a thousand-year period at the end of the age when Christians will reign with Christ on earth literally.

It will not serve our purpose here to delve into the many ramifications of this millennial theory. There are many versions of it, and each version is usually related to an elaborate eschatological program. There are many books available delineating these various millennial positions.[1] It would only confuse the issue to go into the details of these theories here.

Instead, let us share with the reader what we see in this highly figurative picture. I see it as another picture of the celebration of victory, but a special feature of that celebration. A time is coming in the economy of God when He will give special recognition to those of His redeemed children who have been called on to pay the supreme price in their service for the Lord. Whether or not the celebration will last a thousand years is of little importance. Even if it should be a thousand years, that is only a moment in the light of eternity. I am inclined to think that the reference to a thousand years is symbolic like most of the other numbers in the Book of Revelation. It simply signifies an appreciable time in which the martyred saints shall receive special recognition. The reference here is not to all Christians, but only to "the souls of them that were beheaded for the witness of Jesus" (Rev. 20:4). Actually, if one insists on being literal, this recognition would be limited to the martyred saints of the Domitian era; however, the principle may be applied to include *all* who have been martyred for their faith in Christ. Neither is there anything in this text to suggest that this thousand-year reign will be on earth.

There is nothing unfair or unusual about this special recognition of the martyrs. We human beings are accustomed to doing precisely this. Every year we set aside a day here in America called "Memorial Day." On this day we pause to pay special tribute to those who have given their lives in keeping our nation free from its enemies. We do this gladly. Even so has God made arrangements for a time at the end of the age when all of us who have not been called on to give our lives in death because of our faith in Christ will stand aside for a season while we pay special tribute to those who have. This will be an exciting and meaningful part of our celebration of victory at the end of the age. It seems, from the picture John gives to us here, that these martyred saints will have the privilege of trying on their resurrected bodies first. Should I never be called on to pay this supreme price in my service to my Lord on earth, I will gladly take my seat in the background while we all give special tribute to those who have.

The final feature of the celebration will be the privilege of sitting in the grandstand while the old commander-in-chief of the forces of evil, the devil himself, will be brought out of his cell in the bottomless pit and turned loose to rant and rave for a brief season. Thinking that he is free again to fight against the saints, he gathers his cohorts to make an advance on these redeemed gathered in the stands, but before he is able to harm a hair on the head of any saint, the heavenly security guard pounces on him with lightning speed, and he is cast into the lake of fire and brimstone with all of his earthly associates.

A shout of doxology rises up from the saints gathered in the stands, being assured that the old Dragon will be around no more to molest or harm them. This is what John refers to as the battle of Gog and Magog (Rev. 20:8). It is a mock battle, not a real one. There was never a shot fired from Satan's gun. It was simply the final feature of a series of significant celebrations of victory. All of these will transpire at the end of the age, but it would be unwise for us to try to fit them into a chronological order.

The last episode in the drama of redemption (Rev. 20:11-22:5) has to do with the state of the redeemed after the celebration is over. It is a beautiful picture symbolized by a heavenly tabernacle, a holy city, and a gorgeous garden. We shall not pursue these pictures further since it would carry us beyond the end time. The end time for the redeemed will be incredibly exciting, issuing into an eternity of blessedness.

16
THE COMPOSITE PICTURE

Having studied the eschatological picture as revealed by Jesus, Paul, Peter, and John, it remains for us to gather up the various aspects into one composite picture of the end time. There is the temptation to make it all fit into a detailed chronological schedule. Many have succumbed to this temptation. The result is a conglomerate of dates, events, and schedules that have boggled the minds of many Christians. It has become the battleground for hotly contested theological controversies. Through the processes of "eisegesis" (reading into the scripture that which is not really there) elaborate and fantastic schemes have been worked out.

Considering only what we believe to be clearly taught in the New Testament—in particular the passages which have been examined in this study—we shall attempt to give a composite picture. According to these passages there are thirteen events related to the end time. Since we have already made a somewhat detailed study of these events in our "exegesis" of the various eschatological passages, we shall list these events here only in broad outline.

The first two evidently come first from the standpoint of chronology. The others, however, cannot be fixed into a timetable. We know that they are all related to the end time, but we have no scriptural basis for putting them into any kind of a chronological order. In fact, several of them may occur simultaneously, but all of them are a part of the eschatological picture given to us in the New Testament.

The first two conditions to expect in the end time are these: an alarming increase of false prophets and antichrists and a consequent period of great tribulation for God's people. It could well be a period of seven years, but I find nothing in the New Testament to verify or confirm this supposition. Some seem to find a reference to the seven years of tribulation in Revelation 11, but if there is any reference here to a seven-year tribulation period it is extremely vague.

The central event of the end time is the return of Christ to this earth in glory and victory. Of this we can be sure. Nearly every page of the New Testament points to this climactic event. This is the focal point of all eschatology.

Related to this climactic event of the end time, a number of other events will take place. In what chronological order we would not dare to predict. We merely mention the fact that these events will occur in connection with the return of Christ. One would be the dissolution of this earth as we know it now. This material universe will be destroyed. It was not designed to be eternal. As Peter reminds us, it will melt with fervent heat. God has created it, and when He has accomplished His purpose in it, He will destroy it.

At the coming of Christ there will also be a resurrection of the bodies of the redeemed. The graves shall give up their dead, and these bodies which have decayed into dust will rise to newness in glory. The bodies of those still living will be changed into bodies of glory.

There will also be the final overthrow of Satan and his kingdom. The conflict of the ages will come to a climactic end when God empties His seven bowls of wrath upon the kingdom of Satan. In spite of his last-ditch effort, he will go down in ignominious defeat and humiliation.

Somewhere in this end time there will be a great and final judgment. Some Bible scholars seem to see three or four separate judgments separated by time periods. There are a number of different pictures of final judgment to be found in the New Testament, but my study persuades me to believe that there will be only one final judgment which may have several different features. It will be a time of official consignment and official rewards.

Somewhere in the consummation of the age there will be a time and place for tremendous celebrations of victory. One part of it will be in the form of a heavenly choir concert singing songs of victory. Another will be that magnificent wedding in the courts of heaven when the Lamb shall be married to His Bride, the Church. Whether it is before or after the wedding makes little difference, but somewhere in the program of celebration there will be a triumphal procession through the streets of the New Jerusalem, in which all of the redeemed will be riding white horses following our blessed Lord on His white steed.

One of the most significant features of the celebration will be the time of special recognition for the martyred saints. All the rest of us will joyfully take a back seat while we take time to honor those who have been called on to make that supreme sacrifice for their faith in Christ.

The celebration will be climaxed as we sit in the heavenly stadium to witness the official consignment of Satan himself to the lake of fire. A doxology of praise will rise up from the camp of the saints as they see their arch-enemy, who had pursued and oppressed them all through the journey of life here on earth, officially condemned to the fires of eternal hell.

Following these days, or maybe years or even millennia, of celebration, God's redeemed people will settle down in a state of eternal bliss, forever worshiping and having fellowship with their Lord who became their Savior while they were on earth.

There is more than the satisfaction of curiosity in this study of eschatology. It is a strong source of inspiration and courage as we face the future in our struggle against the forces of evil in our world. With the apostle Paul we can shout: "Therefore, my beloved brethren, be ye steadfast, unmoveable, always abounding in the work of the Lord, forasmuch as ye know that your labour is not in vain in the Lord" (1 Cor. 15:58).

Footnotes

Chapter 1

1. A. B. Bruce, *The Training of the Twelve* (New York & London: Hodder and Stoughton, n.d.), 326-340.
2. John A. Broadus, *The American Commentary: Matthew* (Philadelphia: American Baptist Publication Society, n.d.), 479-482.
3. G. Campbell Morgan, *The Gospel According to Matthew* (New York: Fleming H. Revell Co., 1929), 271-285.
4. C. H. Lenski, *The Interpretation of St. Luke's Gospel* (Columbus, OH: The Wartburg Press, 1946).
5. W. A. Criswell, *Expository Notes on the Gospel of Matthew* (Grand Rapids, MI: Zondervan Publishing House, 1961), 129-141.
6. Ray Summers, *The Life Beyond* (Nashville: Broadman Press, 1959).
7. Broadus, Ibid., 480.

Chapter 2

1. G. C. Berkouer, *The Return of Christ* (Grand Rapids, MI: William B. Eerdmans, 1972), 245.
2. *The Scofield Reference Edition*
3. Clarence Larkin, *Dispensational Truth* (Clarence Larkin Estate, 1927).
4. Louis T. Talbot, *God's Plan of the Ages* (Grand Rapids, MI: William B. Eerdmans, 1974).
5. J. Dwight Pentecost, *Prophecy for Today* (Grand Rapids: Zondervan Publishing House, 1961).
6. Criswell, Ibid.
7. For other opinions and interpretations of the millennium see the following:

    J. Dwight Pentecost, *Prophecy for Today* (Grand Rapids: Zondervan Publishing House, 1961).

    John F. Walvoord, *Daniel: The Key to Prophetic Revelation* (Chicago: Moody Press, 1971).

    Charles Caldwell Ryrie, *A Survey of Bible Doctrine* (Chicago: Moody Press, 1972).

    George E. Ladd, *Commentary on the Revelation of John* (Grand Rapids, MI: William B. Eerdmans, 1972).

    Anthony A. Hoekema, *The Bible and the Future* (Grand Rapids, MI: William B. Eerdmans, 1979).

    Robert Clouse, *The Meaning of the Millennium* (Downers Grove, IL: Inter-Varsity Press, 1977).

Chapter 3

1. John Calvin, *Calvin's Commentaries* (Grand Rapids, MI: William B. Eerdmans, 1959), re: Matt. 24:28.
2. Alexander Maclaren, *Christ in the Heart* (New York: Macmillan & Co., 1887), 103.

Chapter 5

1. Edward H. Plumptre, *New Testament Commentary for English Readers*, 1877.
2. Morgan, Ibid., 280-295.
3. Ibid., 293.
4. Op. cit., 503
5. Op. cit., 510.

Chapter 7

1. Op. cit., Vol. V on 1 and 2 Thessalonians, 55, 56.

2. Summers, Ibid., 58.
3. Ibid., 56.

Chapter 8

1. Stevens, Ibid., 91.
2. Ibid., 91.
3. Frederick Godet, *Clark's Foreign Theological Library* (Edinburgh, Scotland: T. & T. Clark, 1881).
4. B. H. Carroll, *An Interpretation of the English Bible* (New York: Fleming H. Revell Co., 1913), Vol. 9.
5. Op. cit., 133.

Chapter 9

1. T. C. Edwards, *Commentary on the First Epistle to the Corinthians*, on 15:44.
2. E. P. Gould, *An American Commentary* (Philadelphia: American Baptist Publication Society, n.d.), Vol. 6, 139.

Chapter 10

1. Charles B. Williams, *The Williams Translation of the New Testament* (Chicago: Moody Press, 1952).

Chapter 11

1. N. M. Williams, *The American Commentary*, 108.

Chapter 12

1. Perry F. Webb, *Doves in the Dust* (Nashville: Broadman Press, 1953), 103.

2. George Adam Smith, *The Forgiveness of Sins* (New York & London: Hodder & Stoughton, n.d.), 121-138.
3. Op. cit., 18.
4. C. S. Lewis, *Christian Behaviour* (New York: The Macmillan Co., 1960).

Chapter 13

1. Summers, Ibid., 145.
2. Op. cit., Sept. 1960.

Chapter 14

1. W. T. Conner, *The Epistles of John* (New York: Fleming H. Revell, 1929), 88-105.
2. Henry A. Sawtelle, *The American Commentary*, on John 2:18, 19.
3. A. Plummer, *The Cambridge Bible* (Cambridge, England: Cambridge University Press, 1894), on 1 John 2:18, 19.
4. H. E. Dana, *The Epistles and Apocalypse of John* (Dallas: Baptist Book Store, 1937), 40.
5. Op. cit., 194.

Chapter 15

1. See list of authors given under note 7 in Chapter 2.

Ordering Information

Copies of *What's Next?* may be ordered for $8.95 per copy plus $2.00 for postage & handling from:

C. E. Colton
8302 Midway Road
Dallas, Texas 75209
(214) 352-3333

or they may be ordered from the Baptist Book Store.

Other books available by C.E. Colton

Meditations on the 23rd Psalm . . . . $5.00 plus $2.00 p&h
The Faithfulness of Faith . . . . . . $5.00 plus $2.00 p&h
A Good God and an Evil World . . . $5.00 plus $2.00 p&h
Laugh, Lament, and Learn . . . . . . $5.00 plus $2.00 p&h